A Possible
Anthropology

ANAND PANDIAN

A Possible
Anthropology

Methods for
Uneasy Times

Duke University Press

Durham and London

2019

Printed in the United States of America on acid-free paper ∞
Designed by Courtney Leigh Baker
Typeset in Whitman and Avenir by Copperline Book Services

Library of Congress Cataloging-in-Publication Data
Names: Pandian, Anand, author.
Title: A possible anthropology : methods for uneasy times /
Anand Pandian.
Description: Durham : Duke University Press, 2019. |
Includes bibliographical references and index.
Identifiers: LCCN 2019006367 (print)
LCCN 2019016267 (ebook)
ISBN 9781478004370 (ebook)
ISBN 9781478003113 (hardcover : alk. paper)
ISBN 9781478003755 (pbk. : alk. paper)
Subjects: LCSH: Anthropology. | Anthropology—Philosophy. |
Anthropology—Methodology.
Classification: LCC GN33 (ebook) | LCC GN33 .P363 2019 (print) |
DDC 301—dc23
LC record available at https://lccn.loc.gov/2019006367

COVER ART: *Spiff*, 2008.
© Judith Selby Lang and Richard Lang.

For Don, Lawrence,
Stefania, Paul,
teachers in
anthropology

CONTENTS

Introduction

An Ethnographer among the Anthropologists

Should I stay or should I go? In the spring of 2018, the indigenous Métis scholar Zoe Todd posted a pained reflection on the state of affairs in anthropology. She had trained in the discipline and served in a university department for several years. The experience, she found, had been exhausting: "To be honest, this work wears away at my cells, my fibres, my bones."[1]

It wasn't just the pressures of an academic job that Todd had in mind. There were also the uncomfortable realities of a field that prided itself on its commitment to social critique. The subtle racism that treated people from elsewhere as objects of study, rather than thinkers and theorists in their own right. The persistence of colonial relations of power and knowledge in the formal structures of the discipline. An impatience with creative and experimental efforts to confound its elitism and hierarchy. "When your body, and your body of work, do not fit neatly into the categories provided, you become a problem," the young anthropologist noted. Who could blame her for thinking to go?

I found myself vexed by Todd's reflections when I encountered them that spring on the blog Anthro{dendum}. Like her and many others, I was drawn into anthropology some years ago by a desire for social transformation. I too had come to see, over the years, how easily this ambition could be reduced to a vehicle for personal advancement. Still, I couldn't shake the sense of anthropology's radical promise. I could hardly think of a more profound way of opening up the space of human possibility. This was a prospect that seemed to keep surfacing, wherever the field's lessons drifted about in the world. In fact, I had seen firsthand how Todd's own work could make this happen.

There was a paper she gave at the 2016 meeting of the American Anthropological Association (AAA). It was a somber and unsettled gathering, clouded by the recent presidential election in the United States. The typical lightness of corridor chatter among old friends and colleagues had given way to expressions of grief and disbelief. I remember stepping into a bathroom stall at the convention center in Minneapolis. On the floor below the toilet was a rainbow-colored flyer printed with just one word, Sapiens. The tableau seemed to capture the state or perhaps the fate of the species at that moment, as many here saw it. You could feel it in the hallways, the sense of aspirations to flush and bid goodbye.

Around the corner, Todd was speaking at a session on indigenous ontology. The hall was packed that afternoon, a basket passing from row to row to gather contributions for the Dakota Access Pipeline struggle. Todd also spoke of oil, but in a highly unusual and moving manner. She talked about her home territory in Alberta, the rivers of the Lake Winnipeg watershed and the threats they faced from petroleum pollution. Could one meet such destructive developments with a spirit of kindness? Calling on the Cree idea of *wahkohtowin*, an enveloping relatedness, Todd claimed a kinship with the ancient and forgotten beings whose remains had since become that oil. "The bones of dinosaurs and the traces of flora and fauna from millions of years ago," she said, "act as teachers for us, reminding us of the life that once teemed here."[2]

Who was this "us" that the anthropologist invoked? Perhaps it was her Métis people alone. And yet, by asserting these responsibilities for human, piscine, and even petroleum kin, by sketching an ethic of tenderness to meet them all with care, she seemed to be calling on all of us in that crowded hall to deepen and nurture our moral sensibilities. Her words conveyed the sense that even in a most disturbing moment, this spirit of kinship could be ours to share, that it could make for a kind of response. It was an unexpected opening, this horizon of possibility, something palpable and present in the room that day. To me, it felt like an instance of genuine hope, even in the face of dispiriting circumstance.

"I think it would be a real tragedy for our discipline if we lost your voice," I told Zoe in the summer of 2018, when we had the chance to converse about that paper, about anthropology, about the frustrations on her mind of late. She told me about her ill-fated undergraduate adventures in biology, and the scientist who first suggested she pursue anthropology: "You seem to really care about people." She talked about her love of teaching, the indigenous thinkers who inspired her practice, and the hardships faced by women of color in the academy.

"I was attracted to anthropology because I thought of it as a very expansive and plural space," Zoe said. "In its best iterations, anthropology is a space of being in the world together, allowing for different understandings of our being. Can we find a way to be kinder and gentler toward one another, at a time when everything is pushing us to be harder and sharper?"

"What would make you want to stay?" I asked. "What do you think would make anthropology more habitable, more hospitable?"

"The possibility of it being more collaborative," she replied, "a space that's willing to break down walls, that's willing to play. We're in the middle of what could be a very serious ending, the end of what we know as human existence. If there's ever been a time for us to play, to be fearless, it's now. The trouble is that the old structures are just clinging for dear life. You can feel the bony white hands of the forefathers trying to claw us back. How do we break that grasp and allow ourselves to float into the wide blue ocean?"

What is possible is never easy to discern. But this is a task all the more imperative now, in this time of hard lines, stubborn limits, and spiraling questions about the future of that being to whom we devote ourselves in anthropology, the human. In the effort to think beyond the impasses of the present, I argue in this book, the discipline has essential resources to contribute. Anthropology teaches us to seek out unseen faces of the world at hand, to confront its openness through experience and encounter, and to take these openings as seeds of a humanity to come. These are methods both ethical and practical, ways of being as much as ways of doing. They are the elements that sustain the critical promise of the field.

To fully realize this promise, though, we have to do more than to accept the field as it is given. For when we think and work in anthropology, we take in its problems as well as its prospects. And as scholars on the edges of the discipline—courageous individuals like Todd and many others—have attested in recent years, the colonial and racist violence that gave rise to the field remains with us even now. What to do in the face of this ambiguous heritage? As with any social field, dominant tendencies in anthropology are always crosscut by residual and emergent elements, to borrow terms from Raymond Williams.[3] The challenge lies in identifying and expanding the scope for what remains on the threshold of possibility.

As anthropologists, we have a method to do just this: ethnography, a practice of critical observation and imagination, an endeavor to trace the outlines of a possible world within the seams of this one. I am an anthropologist; this is the world where I spend much of my time. Some time ago, however, it struck me that I didn't have the best sense of this milieu, of either its serious pitfalls or its real potential. I began to look at this familiar intellectual scene with an ethnographic eye. Eventually, a book took shape, one that grew from avid conversation and collaborative exploration.

Take what follows as an ethnographic encounter with anthropology, an effort to grasp what this field does in the world, with an eye to what it might yet be. This book pursues the vision of a possible anthropology, one to meet the challenge of uneasy times, one willing to set sail with its most imaginative kin.

"SOMETIMES IT IS the truth of the possible as opposed to the actual that needs to be conveyed," Lisa Stevenson writes in a luminous meditation on life and death in the Canadian Arctic.[4] The insight is one that anthropology ought to know well. Every so often, the discipline passes through another moment of radical reinvention, turning away from what lies at hand with an eye to the promise of a distant horizon. This is much more than the symptom of a fickle disposition. There are few intellectual enterprises as profoundly committed to addressing the acute and ever-changing challenges of the world in which we find ourselves. And there is also the slippery and elusive nature of that being at the heart of our inquiries, that creature we call *anthropos*. How could we possibly find an end to its pondering?

For anthropology is the endeavor to conceive a humanity yet to come. To be sure, we work closely and carefully with people lodged in concrete circumstances, with refugees and migrants stranded at international borders, with farmers struggling against the expropriation and contamination of their lands, with scientists and technicians putting experimental infrastructure into motion. And yet, wherever we go and whomever we seek out in curiosity or solidarity, the stories we bring back are only worth telling when they complicate the humanity of those we share them with. "In the act of inventing another culture, the anthropologist invents his own," the late Roy Wagner wrote.[5] Anthropology is a venture in cultural transformation as much as cultural representation, an effort to unsettle and remake what would seem to be given in human being. Humanity is less our object than our medium, a quality we work on and with.

This is, no doubt, a uniquely difficult time to embrace the human as a mode of being and a locus of inquiry. On the one hand, we see a surge of nativist politics around the globe, the repudiation of appeals to a common humanity and the defense instead of racial and national boundaries. On the other hand, the quickening tempo of ecological crises calls us to think beyond the human as a species, and to confront instead our entanglement with the countless other living beings we share this planet with. Like so many other disciplines in the humanities and social sciences, anthropology has been swept of late into diverse currents of posthumanist criticism, rightly devoted to challenging the idea of Homo sapiens as the perfection of terrestrial life.

And yet, it is worth remembering that the human in anthropology has never been a marker of species alone. Humanity is also a horizon of moral aspiration, an impetus to conceive and pursue a common life in profoundly expansive—albeit often controversial—terms. For Johann Gottfried Herder, an eighteenth-century thinker crucial to the origins of anthropology, the *Humanität* of humans lies in their capacity for sympathizing with the condition of beings unlike themselves; as he wrote in his *Outlines of a Philosophy of the History of Man*, "Nature has formed man most of all living creatures for participating in the fate of others."[6]

What would it take to pursue such sympathy as a real possibility—for us, for those we learn from, those for whom we write and teach? This precisely is the promise of experience in anthropology, a promise I explore in this book as an anthropologist but also as an ethnographer in the company of my peers. I rely on "the connection, intellectual and emotional, between observer and observed," essential to the ethnographic enterprise, as Ruth Behar has described it.[7] Think through things as they erupt and evolve, wa-

Border fence between the United States and Mexico, Playas de Tijuana.

gering they will land you in the midst of novel ideas; attune yourself to the travails of others, with the faith that such exposure will bring new lessons; give yourself over to the circumstances of some other life, hoping to find yourself taken beyond the limits of your own. These methods are essential to anthropology's pursuit of humanity as a field of transformative possibility, and they shape, in the pages that follow, how I engage with the discipline and the working lives of its practitioners.

Such aspirations cannot help but unsettle and displace. We dwell, as Anna Tsing suggests, in a "strange new world" of precarious prospects and disturbed settings for life, one that asks us to "stretch our imaginations to grasp its contours."[8] Anthropology can help with this task, for this is an enterprise both deeply empirical and highly speculative, tacking between close attention to what is and sweeping imagination of what else might also be. It is no accident that ethnography, our signal form of practice and expression, shares so much with literary genres like fiction, memoir, and travelogue. Like those endeavors, our stories can also lead far from the confines of some way of life somewhere, trailing individuals, deeds, and their consequences from one world into another, yielding visions of a possible life held unexpectedly in common.

Everything turns, therefore, on how we think between the various forms of encounter that make for anthropology: fieldwork to be sure, as we will see, but also other domains of tangible experience like the ethnographic text and classroom, or the public world of politics and cultural expression, all of which are implicated in the protean force of good description. Occult powers of metamorphosis pulse through these realms, let loose in the form of vivid stories, images, and sounds. Think of how Zora Neale Hurston recalls a white Voodoo priest of Port-au-Prince in her 1938 memoir of the Caribbean, *Tell My Horse*: "As he spoke," she writes, "he moved farther and farther from known land and into the territory of myths and mists. Before our very eyes, he walked out of his nordic body and changed. Whatever the stuff of which the soul of Haiti is made, he was that. You could see the snake god of Dahomey hovering about him. Africa was in his tones. He throbbed and glowed. He used English words but he talked to me from another continent. He was dancing before his gods and the fire of Shango played about him."[9]

Why tarry with such spirits? It matters, what they can do to us and those we introduce them to. The stakes of expression in anthropology verge on the ontological, beckoning toward a recasting of reality as such. Worries abound now regarding the dangers posed by "alternative facts" and "post-truth" fictions in the halls of official power. But let us acknowledge that the plane of the real can tilt far more wildly and profoundly with any good story of ours. "Full-bored ethnographic writing," as Kathleen Stewart observes, "tries to let the otherwise break through, to keep it alive, to tend it."[10] An ethnography is magical by nature, founded on the power of words to arrest and remake, to reach across daunting gulfs of physical and mental being, to rob the proud of their surety and amplify voices otherwise inaudible. Now more than ever, it would seem, we will need these dark arts of expression.

A FEW YEARS AGO, I had the chance to work on a book together with my grandfather, the story of his century of life.[11] The day after we released the book in the southern Indian city of Madurai, I was invited to give a talk about anthropology to local members of the Tamil Nadu Progressive Writers Association. More than a hundred amateur folklorists and anthropologists — teachers, shopkeepers, activists, and party workers by trade — crowded into that stifling hall, posing questions of great acuity. What did anthropology owe to folklore? How did our work differ from that of novelists or psychologists? "You are a professor at an American university, but we see you as a researcher hailing from the traditions of this Tamil soil," one man stood up to say, asking whether we ought to understand anthropological knowledge to begin with modern science, or instead with the customs of ordinary people. Unaccustomed to formal lecturing in Tamil, I tried to make sense of the discipline's methods as best as I could. Listening to these exchanges, the Tamil writer I had worked with on my grandfather's story put the lessons of my talk into far more concise and elegant terms than I could have managed. *Alaiyanum, tholaiyanum,* Kamalalayan concluded: "One must wander, one must get lost."

Anthropology today is a much more diverse enterprise than the scholarly discipline that took shape within elite universities in Europe and North America.[12] Acknowledging this broader global trajectory is essential to what Faye Harrison has described as the "larger project for decolonizing and democratizing anthropology."[13] In India, as with so many other places in the modern world, anthropological knowledge played a role in the machinations of colonial power.[14] Given the discipline's birth in the crucible of empire, it is no surprise that many have tried to expose the "mythos of fieldwork"—to borrow a phrase from George Marcus—as a cover for the abuse of vulnerable others, a shameful heritage to overcome.[15] And yet there is too much to lose in disavowing this heritage altogether, for the techniques of anthropology are also widely seen to sustain contrary ways of imagining and inhabiting the contemporary world. What would it take to nurture an anthropology founded on receptivity to difference—the inevitability, indeed, of wandering, of getting lost—rather than its mastery? How to conceive the history of the discipline, the legacy of its patriarchs and past masters, on less despotic terms?

This is a small book of essays on problems of method in anthropology. The essay is an ambulatory form of writing, a walk along a meandering course of ideas.[16] Taken together, these essays follow a path of reflections: on the distant past of anthropology and a way of recovering its contemporary relevance; on the present of our efforts and the practices that orient them; on the futures that motivate anthropological inquiry in moral and political terms. When it comes to matters of method in anthropology, deep histories of inheritance remain essential, as are neglected and forgotten resources for reinvention.[17] In what follows, therefore, I try to think between the apparently brutal empiricism of early anthropology and the most *au courant* of its contemporary speculative turns, between the stodgy old men of structuralism and their feminist critics, between an emergent posthumanism in anthropology and the discipline's Enlightenment heritage. I work against the periodizing impulse that shapes our imagination of the past, against the fantasy that we might finally and fully—if belatedly still—come into presence with the present. For as Nietzsche pointed out long ago, there is a value to being untimely.[18]

These essays draw on what experience I've had in anthropology, gleaned through years spent in the company of Indian farmers, merchants, filmmakers, and others. But their focus lies in the experience of others: a pair of notable figures from the early years of the discipline, a handful of inventive and influential contemporary anthropologists, and a few activists, artists, and writers who work with the powers of anthropological imagination. I tarry among them as an ethnographer of anthropological practice, trying to rely more on the observations of a studied apprentice than on the authoritative voice of judgment.[19] I pursue points of resonance between anthropological works and the lives of their makers, the practical philosophies at stake in the discipline's habits and concerns, and the cultural afterlife of some of its essential ideas. I rely on the power of ethnography to decenter and dissolve the sovereign self, to convey that, as the poet Arthur Rimbaud once put it, *je est un autre*, "I" as only and ever another.[20] What surfaces in these essays is less "the anthropologist as hero," as in Susan Sontag's famous sketch, than the anthropologist as medium in a wider world of thought and implication.[21]

In a recent book, *Reversed Gaze*, the Kenyan anthropologist Mwenda Ntarangwi takes an ethnographic look at the professional life of American anthropology. "I became very much aware of the reality of being such an outsider in anthropology," he writes, describing the experience of gazing out at the people massed at an AAA annual conference. "The noise level took me aback. Everyone was talking at the same time. But above all there was a sea of Whiteness in front of me."[22] Ntarangwi brings into focus hierarchies of race, gender, and privilege that run through this academic field, insights borne out by recent public reflections on precarious employment in academic anthropology, the exploitation of graduate student labor, and other ways that a profession manifestly devoted to social justice manages still to reproduce inequality in many of its fundamental modes of operation.[23]

Vivid accounts of such dynamics at work have provoked serious debates about the future of the profession, and my efforts here are indebted to the lessons of these essential conversations. At the same time, I want to acknowledge that the ethnographic orientation I follow here is a slightly different one. Written in the spirit of an affirmative critique—an approach spelled out most fully in the coda—this book is based on engagements with more unconventional characters and experimental moments, drawing on hopeful encounters and unusual perspectives to try to grasp the field's enduring potential. This can also be put another way: this is an effort to engage ethnographically with the discipline, rather than the profession, of anthropology.[24] Many of the individuals who surface in these pages have places in the profession, while many others present in the book have nurtured affinities with anthropology from beyond its professional bounds. In what follows, I try to bring anthropology's critical promise into focus by thinking back and forth between such positions, between canonical and marginal figures.

The first of these essays explores the practice of empiricism in anthropology, our way of engaging the world at hand. These days, of course, the world at hand is literally in hand, with no more than a casual tap or swipe on a mobile digital portal to whisk yourself immediately elsewhere. It can be confounding, what this proliferation of streams and platforms can do to the sense of a shared reality. And yet, arguably, anthropology too is devoted to such a perspective on the real: to an empirical world more elusive than the givenness of the here and now, its actuality always open to critical shades of virtual presence and possibility. I develop this argument with close attention to two important figures in early anthropology: Bronisław Malinowski and Zora Neale Hurston. Their respective practices of fieldwork and writing reveal unexpected forms of kinship between a founding father of a manifestly scientific anthropology and a renegade African American writer, consigned to turning her studies of black folklore into fiction. What their work brings into focus, I argue, is ethnography's commitment to the expressive powers of magic, myth, and metaphor, to the conjure of realities otherwise unseen.

The second essay argues that anthropology is founded on a method of experience. Clarity regarding method has been a notoriously difficult matter in the discipline. These challenges have much to do with the inclination to think and work amid the flux of circumstance, which is often seen to compromise any effort to secure a sense of how exactly we do what we do. Here, as a way of tackling this problem, I devote ethnographic attention to four domains of practice essential to the doing of anthropology: reading, writing, teaching, and fieldwork. I explore these practices in the company of four anthropologists with diverse intellectual lineages and empirical interests: the structuralist and mythographer Claude Lévi-Strauss; the phenomenologist and writer Michael Jackson; the economic anthropologist of Africa

Jane Guyer; and the scholar of science and ecology Natasha Myers. Lingering in their studies and offices, passing with them in and out of classrooms and field sites, I trace shared ways of working with the unexpected and its lessons. I examine how the transformative force of encounter can pass onward from domain to domain, carrying the metamorphic charge of the unknown through diverse forms of activity and expression. Anthropology works through such experience of a field, I argue, as a means of working on the experience of those who encounter it. What distinguishes the discipline is this unity of process and endpoint, method and object, means and ends.

The third essay returns to the theme of a humanity yet to come. The essay considers the moral and political stakes of anthropology in this time of grave concerns regarding the human as such, in this era increasingly known by the name of the Anthropocene. I ask whether recent calls for anthropological attention beyond the human have forfeited too quickly the idea of humanity as a horizon of moral and political transformation. Anthropology has long had resources, I argue, to think of nature and culture in nondualistic terms. The abiding relevance of this heritage can be seen in the way that anthropological imagination is exercised in fields beyond the proper limits of the profession. The essay takes up three such fields—politics, art, and fiction—for ethnographic examination, tracking the pursuit of a more expansive sense of humanity by indigenous activists at the 2016 World Conservation Congress; in the efforts of two American artists to conjure the future imprint of our plastic obsessions; and in the modes of being and expression inspired by the novels of Ursula K. Le Guin. By looking back at anthropology through the mirror of such extrapolations, I argue, we may grasp something new in the pragmatic value of that now-vexed idea of ours, culture. Anthropology is less the study of culture as an object of understanding, than the culture or cultivation of humanity as a method of change.

EACH OF THE expressive practices examined in this third essay unfolds in the wake of some catastrophe, a tragic apotheosis of human conceit: in the aftermath of the colonial dispossession of native land and livelihood, or in an earth of the distant future, long past the toxic bustle of the present. What does it mean, in the face of such historical or speculative evidence, to stay with humanity as a horizon of aspiration? We may find the imprint here of what Lauren Berlant calls "cruel optimism . . . the condition of maintaining an attachment to a significantly problematic object," a bind that anthropology also shares in its persistent attention to a vexing humanity.[25] Anthropologists do their work now in the midst of many rival claims about the scope of human possibility: the "radical humanism" of antiracist or anti-imperialist critics calling for the belated fulfillment of a promise of freedom; the "posthumanism" of those who find machines and their networks engulfing the domain of human agency; the "compostism" of ecological thinkers like Donna Haraway, who suggests that the human finds its greatest potential as humus, fermenting alongside countless other living beings.[26] In the face of such diverse concerns, can the stubborn humanism of anthropology be understood as anything other than retrograde?

These questions came up one afternoon in a discussion of an early draft of this book at the University of California, Berkeley.[27] "What is there to glorify in anthropology?" one student asked pointedly. Another participant, Fatima Mojaddedi, rightly challenged the buoyancy of what she'd read here, recounting the circumstances of her own fieldwork in Kabul:

> What does it mean to privilege metaphor, or the magic of words in ethnography, in a place where people can die for speaking metaphorically? Or for using forms of speech considered dangerously irrational? This is a place where America has been engaged in warfare now for over fifteen years, where devastation ranges from the cultural and linguistic to the infrastructural and corporeal. A place where, for some people, the failure of the political and the imposition of a liberal democracy that champions the human is both a crisis of imagination and a crisis of language.

What Mojaddedi said of life in Kabul was moving and profound, and it took time to take in the force of her description, to try to imagine, as she encouraged us to do, the arguments I had made from the wrenching perspective of that scene. Much later, it struck me that she had spoken in a spirit deeply resonant with the idea of anthropology that this book tries to put forward. She had sketched the conditions of a starkly different form of human existence, and she asked what it would take for anthropology to respond to this difference, in all its troubling particularity. She brought the conversation into the register of an ethnographic encounter. Her words put the limits of our humanity at stake, those of us gathered around that seminar table in California. There was no obvious reply to make, only a renewed impetus for attention and reflection.

"We must not conclude that everything which has ever been linked with humanism is to be rejected," Michel Foucault reflected, "but that the humanistic thematic is in itself too supple, too diverse, too inconsistent to serve as an axis for reflection."[28] Writing as a philosopher and historian, weighing various ways of grasping the relevance of the Enlightenment for the present, Foucault proposed "critique" as an alternative principle of thought, the effort "to separate out, from the contingency that has made us what we are, the possibility of no longer being, doing, or thinking what we are, do, or think."[29] Anthropology too involves such critique, I argue in the coda to this book: critique of humanity, pursuit of humanity as axis of reflection, "a practical critique that takes the form of a possible crossing-over."[30] The uniqueness of anthropology lies in its insistence on the openness of the human, an idea pursued in the discipline with greater consistency and tenacity than in any other field of inquiry. Humanism in anthropology can only be "interminable," as Patrice Maniglier has put it, for this is a practice of thought propelled by the singular conviction that "one does not know yet what the human could be."[31]

Admittedly, the scope of this idea may be difficult to sustain in a time of pressing attacks on the academy as a space of free inquiry, the imposition of ever stricter standards for profitable knowledge, and the erosion of conditions that support such endeavors as means of intellectual and professional livelihood. The future of anthropology as a scholarly vocation is charged with uncertainty, and in such an environment, the eclectic and improvisational nature of the discipline's ways may meet with understandable skepticism. "Employers, legislators, parents, and students demand 'relevant' and 'useful' college degrees," while "industries seek informed and skilled graduates to strengthen our economy," Kathryn Kozaitis notes of the pressures faced by public universities, such as her U.S. campus, Georgia State. She adds, though, that while "the engaged university may be a symptom of neoliberal policies," it can also yield space for the "investigation and amelioration of social problems" through creative anthropological projects.[32]

More than half of the graduate students who responded to a recent survey by the AAA said that they were considering careers in advocacy, human rights, and social justice.[33] Most of them, by some combination of necessity and inclination, will have to take their lessons from the field into careers beyond the academy.[34] Could we approach the "impact factor" of anthropological work—to take just one implacable measure—as a matter not simply of citation, but instead of the social life of the ideas the field puts into motion?[35] A recent study by Felix Stein of anthropologists in Britain found their work motivated indeed by "a desire for social efficacy" more than any other kind of "impact" in the world.[36] And the sense of such public consequence that anthropologists carry, as Didier Fassin has noted, is anchored in the peculiarity of ethnography as a proximate, lively, and immersive form, "the sort of truth that is produced, established, and, in the end, told."[37]

Such ambitions, and the tenuous promise of their realization, make it all the more imperative to convey, as tangibly as possible, the critical value of anthropology as a mode of practical and transformative inquiry, rooted in attentive engagements with the world at hand. In these pages, I take up this challenge as a matter of both argument and narration, seeking to write through a series of unfolding encounters with anthropology at work in the world. Such an effort takes what Angela Garcia calls "writing with care," that is, a form of expression that embraces "the possibility of letting things be vulnerable and uncertain."[38] Ideas are worked out here in the company of others at work, taking shape through immersion in experience and storytelling, leaving some of their dimensions necessarily speculative and conjectural. This way of thinking and writing may be prone to charges of inadequate reason and completion. And yet I can't think of a way to engage more faithfully with a discipline devoted to the value of circumstances as we find them, to the significance of incipient and emergent things.

These essays grow from an aspiration for a creative anthropology, one that shares in the transformative powers of experience and the genesis of worlds. For our discipline can indeed help to nurture what Elizabeth Povinelli has called "the will to be otherwise," the fraught effort to pursue knowledge as a project of ethical transformation, thought as "experiment on the self in the world," method as a way of attuning oneself to "the future already among us."[39] In what follows, I pursue the vision of a possible anthropology, one that may be adequate to the challenge of seeing and thinking beyond the profound fissures and limits of the present. These are times that call for anthropological faith and existential generosity, ways of cultivating sympathy, openness, and care as livable realities.

For the humanity yet to come—now, as always, we will need such anthropology.

CHAPTER ONE

The World
at Hand
Between Scientific
and Literary Inquiry

In 1941, the year before his death, Bronisław Malinowski began writing his final book, a study entitled *Freedom and Civilization*. He was teaching then at Yale, and the United States was about to plunge into the Second World War. "What we are now fighting for is nothing short of the survival of culture and humanity," Malinowski wrote.[1] Totalitarian forces had captivated their populations through powerful rituals of loyalty and submission, relying "essentially on the technique of a magical spell."[2] Here was an uneasy yet crucial lesson to absorb, the anthropologist argued: "In our democratic unpreparedness, we have failed to mobilize spiritually."[3] Democratic societies needed to envision a compelling future beyond this time of war, and here they could turn to the social sciences for help in understanding and cultivating the value of freedom. "Ours is an age," Malinowski wrote, "where faith must be in harmony with reason."[4]

While Malinowski worked out these ideas in Connecticut, another notable writer with roots in anthropology, Zora Neale Hurston, spent a few months in Southern California. Working on an autobiography, she too had warfare and social conflict on her mind that year. Hurston, though, was far less sanguine about the promise of scientific understanding. "It is as if we were children playing in a field and found something round and hard to play with," she wrote. "It may be full of beauty and pleasure, and then again it may be full of death."[5] Perspective on any social problem could only be partial, tinged always by the shadow of what remained unseen and unknown. "Light is sharply directed on one spot," Hurston mused, "denying by implication that the great unlighted field exists."[6] Grave were the difficulties signaled by this chapter in her memoir, *Dust Tracks on a Road*, one that grappled with the basic task of "seeing the world as it is."

Taken together, these works bring into focus the challenge of thinking with the world at hand, a pursuit fundamental to anthropology. What is at stake here is the kind of empiricism that anthropology demands—what to do, that is, with the *empeiria* (Greek, for experience) of worldly encounters. "Anthropologists do their thinking, talking and writing in and with the world," Tim Ingold has written: "we do our philosophy out of doors."[7] This is a deceptively simple matter, this philosophizing out of doors. For the thinking that we do, in and with the world, always involves a peculiar interplay between close attention and imaginative reach, movement within and beyond the circumstances in which we work. Who wouldn't recognize the tenor of those impossible aspirations that led Hurston to cry out this prayer in *Dust Tracks*? "Lord, give my poor stammering tongue at least one taste of the whole round world, if you please, Sir."

This essay examines the texture of empiricism in anthropology. I focus most closely on these two idiosyncratic figures from the field's early years, Bronisław Malinowski and Zora Neale Hurston. The Polish ethnographer and the African American folklorist make, no doubt, an unlikely pair: one a legendary and canonical presence, and the other a woman who never found her footing in the institutions of the profession—who never had the chance, in fact, to pursue the Ph.D. she hoped to complete at Columbia University in the 1920s. Then of course there is Malinowski's famous cry from his Trobriand diaries—*no more novels!*—and Hurston's own avocation as a pioneering African American novelist. Still, I want to argue, there are striking affinities to pursue between these two writers, contemporaries with each other. In what follows, I pursue these affinities by tacking between the writings of these two figures and the biographical texture of their lives. I try to follow, in the manner of an ethnographer, how their ideas grow from the empirical circumstances of their work. I pay attention to various ways in which these latter details deepen—and sometimes confound—the timbre of their written words.

"The discourse of anthropology is a curious blend of both sorcery and science," Michael Jackson has observed.[8] We tend to think of these endeavors as polar opposites, rival and incommensurable approaches to the density of worldly life: one allied with arts such as magic and poetry, and the other a means of more reliable knowledge about the world. Thinking between figures as distinctive as Malinowski and Hurston, however, brings into focus the space between these two poles. For anthropology's indefatigable champion of fieldwork was much less the stern rationalist we now take him to be. And the literary imagination of the American novelist owed a great deal to her training in field methods.

I follow these threads of affinity as a way of unraveling the reality at stake in anthropological inquiry. What we find is an empirical world more elusive than the givenness of the here and now, its actuality always open to critical shades of virtual presence and possibility. Anthropology can still happen, nevertheless, in such a world, because ours is an empirical venture that depends on the expressive powers of magic, myth, and metaphor, the conjure of realities otherwise unseen.[9]

OF ALL THE ACADEMIC departments at the American university where I work, there is only one that declares to every visitor where else on the planet their members might be. I have in mind the world map prominently displayed just outside the door to the anthropology office at Johns Hopkins University, which marks faculty and student field sites around the world. The absence of such a map elsewhere on campus is somewhat surprising: there are many other programs here—earth and planetary sciences, global public health, and so on—with a notable emphasis on field research, that value close attention to the ground-level details of distant places. Yet, wandering from building to building on the campus one crisp winter morning, looking for evidence of such things, I mostly met with puzzled smiles and incredulous looks. "You mean a map of our building?"

Here though in this department—as with so many other anthropology departments around the country—is this map of the world, mounted onto a corkboard in the main hallway, with a multitude of pins and flags in blue, red, and white, marking localities in North and South America, Europe and the Middle East, Africa and Asia. I can't say whether any of us has actually worked in Greenland, as one of the flags presently suggests. But, taken together, these markers cast a different light on hallways lined with closed office doors, as is the case most of the time throughout the university. The map implies something less prosaic about these closed doors than a beleaguered faculty hiding out from students and administrative demands. The implication is that we could actually be elsewhere, on the trail of where our work has taken us.

Of course, this wasn't always the case. Take, for example, this portrait of James G. Frazer buried within his study at Cambridge University, as sketched in a biography of the early anthropologist: "twelve hours a day at his books was quite the usual thing, while fifteen hours was not rare, and I have it on the best authority that he has several times left his library at Trinity College at two in the morning to return to it at eight the same morning."[10] It was precisely this image of a scholar nestled among books that Malinowski and many others would contest as "armchair" anthropology. As Malinowski declared in his Frazer Lecture of 1925, "I shall invite my readers to step outside the closed study of the theorist into the open air of the anthropological field."[11]

This distinction between two radically different environments for thought—closeted study and open-air field—marks one of the most significant features of anthropological knowledge in the early years of the discipline. As with other field sciences, the enterprise of anthropology was at first divided between the analytical work of gentlemen scientists in metropolitan Europe, and the travelers, missionaries, and colonial servants who gathered data for them from places far afield. Amateur observers were exhorted to collect what "facts" they could from the grimy circumstances of colonial frontiers, leaving their interpretation to proper scientists sheltered from the elements. But beginning in the late nineteenth century, newly established tropical field stations and other endeavors in field-based research challenged this division of intellectual labor, insisting on the value of knowledge grounded more closely in empirical circumstances.[12]

For anthropology, an essential moment in the professional consecration of field experience came with the 1898 Cambridge Anthropological Expedition to Torres Straits, led by the Dublin zoologist A. C. Haddon. Relying on their training in psychology and physiology, and a battery of experimental tests, seven British men sought to establish the adaptive responsiveness of their Pacific island subjects to the sensory demands of that environment and its means of subsistence. Among them were Charles Seligman, a physician who later became Malinowski's mentor at the London School of Economics, and W. H. R. Rivers, who would insist, in his remarks on method in the 1912 edition of *Notes and Queries on Anthropology*, that "the abstract should always be approached through the concrete."[13]

Notes and Queries was a fieldwork handbook that Malinowski carried with him and often consulted during his own South Pacific fieldwork a few years later. But in the annals of British anthropology, Malinowski's legendary research in the Trobriand Islands soon eclipsed the groundwork laid down by his forebears and teachers. His preeminent status as an exemplary fieldworker has been ascribed to both a genius for self-promotion and a flair for rhetorical persuasion. His 1922 classic, *Argonauts of the Western Pacific*, as George Stocking has memorably suggested, mythologized and even divinized its anthropologist hero, "the European Jason who brings back the Golden Fleece of ethnographic knowledge."[14] But, at the same time, there is more at stake here than a matter of narrative license. There remains that alchemical mystery at the heart of the juncture between description and theory, ethnography and argument. How does an observation yield an idea?

Take the essay that made Malinowski's reputation as an anthropologist: "Baloma: The Spirits of the Dead in the Trobriand Islands," published in the *Journal of the Royal Anthropological Institute of Great Britain and Ireland* in 1916. The essay was written over several weeks in Melbourne, Australia, during a lengthy interval between two stints of fieldwork in the Trobriand Islands and Papua New Guinea. Reporting on his months spent on the island of Kiriwina, "where he lived among the natives in a tent," Malinowski tackles a series of puzzles concerning the souls or spirits of the deceased in Trobriand culture.[15] How do these *baloma* differ from the ghosts and sorceresses that haunt the outskirts of Trobriand settlements? Where do they go after the death of individuals, and how are they made to return? What role do these spirits of the dead play in the genesis of life, in the magic rituals that make gardens grow, or in the conception of human children? With all such matters, Malinowski notes, "the crude data present almost a chaos of diversity and multiplicity," with the most basic of queries eliciting a bewildering array of responses.[16]

What is the ethnographer to do with such discordant impressions? "Field-work consists only and exclusively in the interpretation of the chaotic social reality," he writes, "in subordinating it to general rules."[17] Given the confidence of this declaration, however, one of the most striking aspects of "Baloma" is the indiscipline of its form. The writing itself would appear to be haphazard, as Malinowski, aiming "to state the difficulties I encountered in my work and the manner in which I tried to cope with them," wends his way through page after page of vivid reminiscences, asides, conjectures, and indulgences that draw the reader deep into the intricacies of an unfamiliar milieu with little sense, at least at first, of what to do with all these details.[18] The anthropologist himself acknowledges so much of what appears in the essay—spanning seventy-eight pages of a journal issue just over two hundred pages in length—as "digression," yet another moment of lingering in the "desperate blind alleys" that mire ethnographic knowledge in the "contradictions and obscurities" of native pronouncements.[19] It is as though the character of Malinowski's own thinking resembles that of his Trobriand informants, working with "ideas . . . in an uncrystallized form, rather felt than formulated."[20]

The essay, in fact, often seeks to underscore such unity between European habits of thought and the thinking of Trobriand Islanders, for "the native mind works according to the same rules as ours."[21] It may seem striking, Malinowski observes, that these are a people who insist that *baloma* rather than fathers are responsible for the conception of a child. But the strangeness of this belief dissipates when the rarity of conception is juxtaposed with the ordinariness here of sexual relations, and the value attributed to the *baloma*'s return.[22] There are, in other words, "social dimensions" that anchor such beliefs and make sense of their complexity: the customs and institutions in which they are embodied, and the social relationships that sustain both orthodox explanations and unusual speculations. And this dense social fabric of explanation, Malinowski insists, is as essential to the work of anthropologists as it is to those they work with: "The observer's own difficulties . . . must be excused on the same account."[23]

We begin to see, with these meditations on the anthropologist's complicity with his subjects, why Malinowski's account of what he learned in the Trobriands must wend its way through the many encounters that yielded these lessons, "bit by bit, through actual experience."[24] There is something deeply misleading about "the cult of 'pure fact,'" he observes, the idea that knowledge only counts as such when purified of its social texture.[25] Rather than leading from the concrete to the abstract, as his mentor W. H. R. Rivers had argued so notably, Malinowski suggests that the concrete itself is already abstract, already laden with incipient ideas and generalities. Whatever we might take as a concrete, empirical "fact" is already an abstraction: "every plan of a village or of grounds, every genealogy, every description of a ceremony—in fact, every ethnological document—is in itself a generalization,"[26] an amalgam of descriptive fidelity and interpretive coherence.

"It is not enough to have the facts right in front of one, the faculty to deal with them must be there," Malinowski writes.[27] To grasp the empirical as already conceptual, a fact as already an idea, if only virtually so: what would it take to attune oneself to this possibility, to learn to engage the actual matter of the world in this manner?[28]

FOR SO MUCH of early anthropology, the world at hand was a colonial world, its lived truths steeped in the reality of racial and political domination. Take the imperial scaffolding for Malinowski's fieldwork in the Trobriands, islands named after an eighteenth-century French explorer and then passed from British to Australian hands in 1905. Malinowski first arrived in Kiriwina on a missionary schooner in 1915, landing on a coral jetty built by prison laborers and borrowing his famous tent from the English resident magistrate overseeing the island. He worked with native men and women who could be jailed for failing to tidy their hamlets or plant coconuts on command, and often sought refuge in the company of local European pearl traders.[29]

At idle moments, Malinowski would toy with the idea of a "new humanism" to supplant Greco-Roman classicism, "in which living man, living language, and living full-blooded facts would be the core of the situation."[30] And yet the reality of colonial Papua constantly cut against the span of this humanistic imagination. "I simply loathe the whole village and all its inhabitants," Malinowski complained in one 1918 letter to his fiancée Elsie Masson, deriding a chiefly informant—covered with soot in ritual mourning for his just-deceased wife—as "black like a chimney sweep or an East End minstrel nigger."[31] The fieldworker confessed a longing to return to the sanctuary of a library, speculating what ethnography might be like among those of his own kind: "sociological observation, if done under different conditions, say in a European community, would have all the charm this work has and none of its loathsome drawbacks."[32]

For as much as Malinowski could dream of "merging with" or "dissolving into" the magnetic seascapes of the South Seas—a recurrent sensation attested by his diaries—such absorption in the landscape was not enough to effect the kind of reasoning that ethnographic fieldwork involved. There was also the challenge of thinking with those other human beings who inhabited this world, that singular exertion that *Argonauts of the Western Pacific* would famously call for, "to grasp the native's point of view . . . to realize *his* vision of *his* world."[33] How could one leap from the idiosyncrasy of such foreign perspectives to the general horizons of anthropological inquiry, from "folk ideas" to "universal ideas," as Malinowski once put it in terms borrowed from the nineteenth-century German ethnologist Adolf Bastian?[34]

Although the anthropologist would insist that "the native mind works according to the same rules as ours," the principle was more difficult to put into practice in actual work with other minds.[35] Witness what Eslanda Goode Robeson, a prominent African American author and activist, reported about her studies in anthropology under Malinowski, Raymond Firth, and others at the London School of Economics in the 1930s. "I soon became fed up with white students and teachers 'interpreting' the Negro mind and character to me," she recalled, reporting on the ideas that prevailed in the classroom: "'The primitive mind cannot grasp the kind of ideas we can; they have schools, but their schools have only simple subjects, and crafts; it's all very different.'"[36]

Nowhere was this impasse between the universal horizons of early anthropology and its stubborn racial parochialism expressed more unjustly than in the case of the American anthropologist and novelist Zora Neale Hurston, who had studied under another foundational figure, Franz Boas, in the 1920s. Now a legendary figure in American letters, Hurston died in neglect in a segregated Florida welfare home in 1960; at the time, all but one of her books were out of print. Hurston had come of age on her own in the early twentieth century, supporting herself through odd jobs and committing to memory whatever books she would encounter in many years of seeking a living in the American South. The publication of a short story in a leading African American magazine took her to New York City in 1925, where, soon thereafter, she pursued anthropology as the first African American student at Barnard College.[37]

"I became Barnard's sacred black cow," Hurston later recalled lightly in her memoir, *Dust Tracks on a Road*.[38] Her initiation into fieldwork came with an assignment for Boas on the streets of nearby Harlem, where she was tasked with measuring the skulls of African American passersby. Boas wanted physical data to refute the idea of a natural inferiority of the Negro mind. Cruelly, however, it was precisely this idea of a racial limit to intellection that would shadow Hurston throughout her career as an anthropologist. When she applied to the Guggenheim Foundation in 1934 to conduct anthropological fieldwork in West Africa, for example, the novelist Fannie Hurst—who had employed Hurston during her first term at Barnard—contributed these words of ambiguous praise: "She is an erratic worker, but in my opinion, a talented and peculiarly capable young woman. She is a rather curious example of a sophisticated negro mind that has retained many characteristics of the old-fashioned and humble type."[39]

What we know of their relationship suggests that Boas was, for the most part, an encouraging mentor to Hurston. In *Dust Tracks*, Hurston writes affectionately of "Papa Franz," telling one racially charged anecdote about an evening when she'd let this nickname slip at a department party. "Of course, Zora is my daughter. Certainly!" the German-Jewish émigré from Westphalia reportedly said—"Just one of my missteps, that's all."[40] In the winter of 1927, Boas secured funding for Hurston to travel through Florida for six months, collecting African American folklore. This first field expedition proved markedly unsuccessful, leading Hurston to cry "salty tears" to her advisor after she returned to New York.[41] Boas felt that the material she gathered repeated what was already known of African American tales, songs, customs, and beliefs. "You remember that when we talked about this matter I asked you particularly to pay attention, not so much to the content, but rather to the form of diction, movements, and so on," he admonished in one letter written to Hurston that year.[42]

In the American cultural anthropology pioneered by Boas, there was always a tension between description and explanation, between attention to individual phenomena and the derivation of general laws that could explain their development. "Boas saw the scientific task as one of progressive probing into a problem now of language, now of physical type, now of art style," Margaret Mead once wrote, describing the "enormous untapped and unknown mass of information" to which Boas directed his students. "No probe must go too far lest it lead to premature generalization—a development which he feared like the plague and against which he continually warned us."[43] These reflections help to make sense of the kind of movement between diverse phenomena that Boas encouraged Hurston to pursue, attention to possible patterns across the range of cultural elements. "When you compare Negro singing and the singing of white people," he continued in that same letter to the novice fieldworker, "it is not so much the musical notation that is different but rather the manner of rendition."[44] The only way to grasp what was truly distinctive in African American folk culture, in other words, was to focus on the *form* of folk expression rather than its contents alone.

In 1928, Hurston began a second and much longer period of fieldwork in the American South, traveling from place to place in a gray Chevrolet and striking up conversations with working men and women in sawmill colonies, phosphate mines, and railway camps in Alabama, Florida, and Louisiana. Correspondence with Boas remained an occasion for comparative reflection—"May I say that all primitive music originated about the drum, and that singing was an attenuation of the drum-beat," she said in one letter from Eau Gallie, Florida, thinking about the vibrant music of the "jook joints" she'd been frequenting.[45] But Hurston was also working quietly toward what she thought of as "general laws" of Negro cultural expression, as she confessed in a letter to one of her closest friends at the time, the poet and playwright Langston Hughes.

She had found, for example, an "angularity in everything," in sculpture, dance, and storytelling. There were notable patterns in spoken diction, such as a redundancy of descriptive terms and customary forms of contraction. And most importantly, despite whatever was said of primitive minds, Hurston was finding a robust creativity in African American culture. "Negro folk-lore is <u>still</u> in the making," she wrote as a seventh "discovery" in her letter to Hughes: "A new kind is crowding out the old."[46]

What method would be suited best to convey this originality?

THE PLACE WHERE Hurston was buried in coastal Florida remained unmarked until 1973, when the writer Alice Walker found the spot in an abandoned graveyard and placed a headstone in tribute to "A Genius of the South." Her epitaph continued with three words recalling Hurston's vocation: "Novelist, Folklorist, Anthropologist."[47] In her lifetime, Hurston had published several celebrated novels, two books of folklore, and countless stories, essays, and works of reportage. But there was always a question of whether her work contributed to the nascent field of anthropology, a question that Hurston herself would ponder. Although a member of the American Anthropological Association, the American Ethnological Society, and the American Folk-Lore Society, she did not receive the funding to pursue doctoral work in anthropology at Columbia University.

Zora Neale Hurston with Rochelle French and Gabriel Brown, Eatonville, Florida, 1935. Prints and Photographs Division, Library of Congress. Courtesy of the Zora Neale Hurston Trust.

There was also the matter of Hurston's influential role in the Harlem Renaissance of the 1920s, a movement of African American creative expression that not only brought an unprecedented cultural prominence to black artists, writers, and dramatists but also scandalized bourgeois American society with its sexual freedoms and libidinal energies. Hurston was a pivotal figure among the Harlem literary pioneers who styled themselves as a defiant "Niggerati," and her stories, plays, and musicals gave her a flamboyant profile very unusual for a student of other cultures. Was she too involved with the sensual life of her subjects to put it forward objectively? "She has neither the temperament nor the training to present this material in an orderly manner," Ruth Benedict pronounced in one arch assessment of Hurston's research in the 1930s.[48]

Expectations of scholarly distance take on a peculiar form when it comes to anthropology, given the undeniably "immersive" nature of fieldwork. Take that contradictory idea of being both within and without the worlds we study, both of these too somehow at the same time, what we have learned to call "participant observation." This unwieldy phrase, James Clifford observes, "serves as shorthand for a continuous tacking between the 'inside' and 'outside' of events: on the one hand grasping the sense of specific occurrences and gestures empathetically, on the other stepping back to situate these meanings in wider contexts."[49] Fieldwork was enshrined as the canonical method of anthropology, with the idea that the significance of things depends on the local contexts that give rise to them, that there is little value to work that does not enter into these local situations. At the same time, however, there is also the idea that this significance can only be grasped ultimately by stepping away from these particular contexts, by recasting them in relation to an analytical framework of greater scale.

The value of a context for understanding, in other words, depends on the existence of an observer who can be lifted from it, who can judge from the outside what was learned inside. Without that foothold on a position beyond our objects of study, Marilyn Strathern writes with regard to the basic assumptions of modern anthropology, there is no support "for their internal integrity, for the way they fit together as parts of a system or have meaning for the actors."[50]

Consider, for example, Hurston's book *Mules and Men*, first published in 1935. Gathering up the black folklore she had collected in the late 1920s, the book begins with Hurston motoring into the African American township of Eatonville, Florida, where she had grown up at the turn of the century. "Well, if it ain't Zora Hurston!" one of the men on the porch of the village store declares, and indeed, such intimacy and familiarity with local life are essential to the spirit of the book. In his brief preface to *Mules and Men*, Boas affirms not once but twice that Hurston has revealed here a "true inner life," observing that "she entered into the homely life of the southern Negro as one of them."[51]

For her own part, Hurston acknowledges that the tales recorded in the book were familiar to her "from the earliest rocking of my cradle." And yet, she writes, "it was fitting me like a tight chemise. I couldn't see it for wearing it." It was only when she had left these "native surroundings" and learned to "see myself like somebody else," at a distance, that she could appreciate the value of this folk heritage. "I had to have the spy-glass of Anthropology to look through at that."[52]

The difference between these two perspectives on a local world, near and far, is registered throughout *Mules and Men*, as Hurston tacks back and forth between vivid re-creations of the tales of Brer Rabbit, Ole Massa, and other familiar characters of black folklore, and her own depiction of the everyday environs—store porch, jook joint, campfire, lakeshore—in which these tales were told.

> Jim Presley spat in the lake and began:
> "Once upon a time was a good ole time—monkey chew tobacco and spit white lime. Well, this was a man dat had a wife and five chillun, and a dog and a cat.
> "Well, de hongry times caught 'em. Hard times everywhere. Nobody didn't have no mo' then jus' enough to keep 'em alive."[53]

Throughout such moments, Hurston weaves artfully between a standard English familiar to white American readers of prose, and a written approximation—"Give us somethin' to wet our goozles wid, and you kin git some lies, Zora"—of black vernacular speech.[54]

These alternations between an inside and outside vantage point persist throughout the first part of the book. Then, however, they give way to a different style of narration, as Hurston turns to the subject of hoodoo in New Orleans. We follow the anthropologist herself as she is taken deeper and deeper into a series of ritual initiations that tarry with occult and capricious forces. Less a guide now than a novitiate, Hurston reports on experiences—"indescribable noises, sights, feelings"—that grow ever more strange and unsettling.[55] By the end of the book, the two distinct voices with which it began, native and anthropologist, have collapsed into one. "I'm sitting here like Sis Cat," she tells us, with diction reserved hitherto for her southern companions, "washing my face and usin' my manners."[56] We too, it would seem, number now among them.[57]

In a letter written to Boas on August 20, 1934, Hurston expressed misgivings about how *Mules and Men* unfolds, its movement between the tales themselves and the ordinary circumstances in which they were told, putting down her lively depiction of the latter as "unscientific matter that must be there for the sake of the average reader." Her scholarly task, she implied, lay in the recording of the folk materials themselves, rather than these recountings of their cultural life: "of course I never would have set them down for scientists to read," she writes with this contextual fabric in mind.[58]

It is hard to know how to interpret these remarks, meant to encourage a powerful academic patron to contribute his stamp of approval to a book crafted with a popular audience in mind. There was no doubt a degree of dissimulation in these self-deprecating words, for *Mules and Men* is written with tremendous fidelity and care, far more than warranted by a capitulation to the expectations of a commercial publisher. Still, these remarks provoke a crucial question, when considered alongside the heady plunge into the depths of black experience that the book demands of its readers. What exactly is context meant to contribute to anthropological understanding?

Anthropology, Roy Wagner has argued, catches us up in something like the Indian philosophical parable of Indra's net, the idea of a net belonging to the emperor of gods. The net's holes are actually jewels, instances not of absence but of infinite presence, each of them rippling with such light that it becomes impossible to say whether each is just one jewel or an image of everything altogether. The net, in its elusive reality, obscures the distinction between figure and ground, object and context, a part and the whole to which it belongs. As does anthropology, Wagner suggests, which seeks ever to unseat its observers from the position in which they judge the world. "You can only get 'into' it," he writes, "by trying to *think* your way out of it."[59]

The task is more complicated, and indeed more unsettling, in other words, than simply stepping back from something to grasp its contours more precisely. Each detail with which we work, writes Wagner, "turns subjectivity inside out," landing us in the heart of things that promise a world unto themselves.[60] Context then, from this vantage point, is less a means of securing our understanding than of displacing its terms altogether. Context, that is, can do something more profound than make sense of what we have found as ethnographers. Like the walls of the rabbit hole into which Lewis Carroll's Alice would tumble, context can mark how deep we've gone.

Hurston was already thinking and working with such possibilities in the early twentieth century, with a degree of philosophical verve that few appreciate still. "I have been amazed by the Anglo-Saxon's lack of curiosity about the internal lives and emotions of the Negroes," Hurston wrote in a cutting 1950 essay called "What White Publishers Won't Print."[61] The viewpoint against which she wrote was one that reduced African Americans to caricatures mounted in a museum diorama, "made of bent wires without insides at all."[62] Her response to such perceptions was not to fill out this inner life, so that one could stand back and admire its depth with patronizing enthusiasm. Instead, her writings pursued the challenge of reimagining the world itself from within these cultural recesses, "from the middle of the Negro out—not the reverse."[63]

Works like *Mules and Men* would find in black folklore a means of recasting the nature of things, the world seen anew from the inside out. "A world is somethin' ain't never finished," God would say in one of these folktales, making butterflies from pieces of earth and sky.[64] What Hurston wanted from such tales—called "lies" by everyone who heard and told them—were resources for the reinvention of reality itself.

MARCH 25, 1918. Bronisław Malinowski is camped on the small island of Gumasila, "a tall, steep mountain with arched lines and great cliffs, suggesting vaguely some huge Gothic monument."[65] Less than two weeks have passed since his final days of fieldwork in the Trobriands. Now, moored briefly among the nearby Amphlett Islands, the anthropologist is hoping for some comparative perspective on the customs of the Melanesians. This day, like so many on this final expedition of his, seems to have been riddled with tensions and frustrations. The men of the island have once again demurred at taking him with them on a *kula* expedition. Passing his time instead with a story by Rudyard Kipling, Malinowski spends the late afternoon rowing around the perimeter of the small island. A glimpse of the towering peak looming above another nearby island leads him to wonder what it will be like to leave Papua for good. The trails of memory always follow such "lines of definite interest, desire, sentiment," he later notes in his diary. Then he adds two more sentences that bring into focus what it means to think with such travails of circumstance. "'Thought takes its impetus from life, not life from thought.' Or else, thoughts are the drifting floats or the buoys which mark the current & it is not they who direct the current but inversely."[66]

Malinowski, Edmund Leach once noted somewhat tartly, had "a bias against abstract theory which kept his imagination firmly earthbound."[67] Say Leach was right about the intellectual orientation of his teacher at the London School of Economics: is there a way of conceiving this earthbound— or even waterbound—imagination as anything but a limitation? Consider, for example, that Malinowski's own doctorate was in the field of philosophy, awarded by the Jagiellonian University in Cracow in 1908. Nietzsche was a significant early inspiration for the young scholar, as were seminars on physics and mathematics. Most consequential for his empiricist bent, however, was the work of the Austrian experimental physicist and psychologist Ernst Mach, a pivotal influence on all of Malinowski's teachers at the Jagiellonian.

Amphlett Islands. Photograph by Bronisław Malinowski, c. 1915–18.
Courtesy of the London School of Economics Library Archives.

Mach's empiricism insisted on the physical reality of thoughts and sensations, taking such subjective phenomena as things among the material elements of the world.[68] In his most significant work of philosophy, the 1905 book *Knowledge and Error*, Mach drew on studies of animal behavior and comparative anthropology to chart something like a natural history of thought. Over time, Mach argued, human thoughts have adapted themselves more and more closely to the facts of worldly experience, offering ever more "economy" or simplicity of explanation. This process yielded the laws of nature known to science, but it also conveyed a more profound lesson, a rupture of the very boundary between mind and world. "If the ego is not a monad isolated from the world but a part of it," Mach wrote, "we shall no longer be inclined to regard the world as an unknowable something."[69] This realization of a deeper affinity between mind and world, in fact, was the very foundation of "real knowledge."

For Mach, the economy of thought served to overcome the difficulties of worldly life, the psychic threat of the unknown, the countless worries faced by a more "primitive" man: "When he hears a noise in the underbrush he constructs there, just as the animal does, the enemy which he fears; when he sees a certain rind he forms mentally the image of the fruit which he is in search of."[70] Malinowski's 1906 doctoral dissertation in philosophy—"On the Principle of the Economy of Thought"—cited these words from Mach, wrestling with the idea that thinking could overcome such travails. For the young Polish scholar, Mach's assumption that "thoughts are expressions of organic life" relied too heavily on Darwin's evolutionary reasoning. His dissertation therefore concluded with a stated impasse between thought and experience: "We do not yet have an empirical basis for a philosophical worldview."[71] It was a tension that Malinowski carried with him a decade later to the South Seas, only to find it dissolved by the trials of fieldwork.

For what these circumstances would reveal was an "organic life" far more open-ended and capricious than the idea of biological adaptation might imply. Malinowski's field diaries from the South Seas document, in painful detail, an exposure to precisely the hazards of embodied experience that his dissertation had examined from a philosophical standpoint. The diaries record a "superirritability and supersensitiveness of mental epidermis," a "feeling of permanently being exposed in an uncomfortable position to the eyes of a crowded thoroughfare."[72] Assailed by recurrent fevers, yelling children, unscrupulous colonials, and the insistent tugs of "lecherous thoughts," Malinowski lamented the way that "my thoughts pull me down to the surface of the world," making into a quixotic ideal the desire "to submerge myself in the deeper, metaphysical stream of life, where you are not swept by undercurrents or tossed about by the waves."[73]

Then too, however, what came through at moments of greater calm was a chance to reconcile thinking with such fluctuations of experience. "Thoughts are the drifting floats or the buoys which mark the current," Malinowski had written that day in Gumasila, as if to suggest that the course of thought could convey the movement of life itself. What emerges from his diary are glimpses of a potential affinity between thinking and living, of attuning one's senses to the conceptual richness of the world at hand. Impressions would indeed come as "waves of new things," tides that would "flow from all sides, break against each other, mix, and vanish."[74] But fieldwork was an apprenticeship in drawing ideas from these tides, in finding resources for thought amid their play. The following morning on Gumasila, as it happens, the anthropologist found the experience to echo his empiricist readings.[75]

To be sure, Malinowski's diaries often revealed an anthropologist wrestling with bodily habits and impulses, castigating himself for practical failures and moral shortcomings.[76] It would be a mistake, however, to dwell on such moments alone as the crucible of fieldwork ideas, as if these ideas depended on a repudiation and overcoming of the circumstances where they appeared. Instead, the spirit of thinking that Malinowski inherited from his philosophical training was less imperious, less antagonistic, committed instead to taking shape through the tugs of experience itself, aiming "to formulate the endless variety of things in the current of a life."[77] As he would observe the following year, in handwritten notes prepared for an informal seminar on philosophy in Melbourne, the truth of a proposition lay in "the quality of an experience" rather than a more distant portrayal of reality.[78]

Fieldwork itself, in other words, could be a kind of empirical philosophy, a worldly basis and foundation for a philosophical outlook. The insights it promised were the only kind of truths worth grasping, Malinowski insisted, those that would surface in the maelstrom of experience. "Philosophy should formulate Truth as we live it," the anthropologist scribbled onto a page of these notes, "not as we think (or more often misapprehend it) at the end of an armchair nap in a metaphysical mood."[79]

BRONISŁAW MALINOWSKI AND Zora Neale Hurston. An unlikely pair, to be sure: a scientist and a novelist, a paragon of rationalism and an artist of fictions, one a founding father of anthropology and the other an illegitimate daughter—in a sense, of course, but still, a very real sense—of another foundational paterfamilias. The tensions between these poles run to the heart of anthropology and its peculiar ways of knowing the world. But there are also certain intriguing resonances between the thinking of these two figures, Malinowski and Hurston. Take, for example, their shared passion for writing. Or even the shape of the world itself, the reality that found expression in their texts.

Haiti, Hurston tells us in her controversial 1938 book *Tell My Horse*, is a land populated by countless Voodoo gods and goddesses. Among them is one she names Erzulie Freida, described by Hurston as "the pagan goddess of love."[80] She writes of Erzulie as a jealous and possessive spirit, demanding a total devotion from the many mortal men she chooses as her husbands. How does a man know that he has been selected by the goddess as a consort? "It usually begins in troubled dreams," Hurston writes. "At first his dreams are vague. He is visited by a strange being which he cannot identify. He cannot make out at first what is wanted of him. He touches rich fabrics momentarily but they flit away from his grasp."[81]

The anthropologist is seeking here to put into words a reality equally elusive, for there is nothing figurative about the intended union: despite the garb of the Virgin Mary in which she is often pictured, what Erzulie pursues is ecstatic sexual contact with her devotees. In one of the book's most moving passages, Hurston intimates that she too has glimpsed something of this impossible coupling:

> There is a whole library of tales of how this man and that was "reclame" by the goddess Erzulie, or how that one came to attach himself to the Cult. I have stood in one of the bedrooms, decorated and furnished for a visit from the invisible perfection. I looked at the little government employee standing there amid the cut flowers, the cakes, the perfumes and the lace covered bed and with the spur of imagination, saw his common clay glow with some borrowed light and his earthiness transfigured as he mated with a goddess that night—with Erzulie, the lady upon the rock whose toes are pretty and flowery.[82]

Hurston's writings, Henry Louis Gates has suggested, are steeped in a "mythic realism, lush and dense within a lyrical black idiom."[83] Passages such as this one from *Tell My Horse* make for vivid and engaging reading. But do such moments of dream and reverie, moments in which the anthropologist herself succumbs to an imaginative drift, signal a rupture of scholarly authority? Empirical rigor in anthropology is often conceived as a fidelity to the evidence of the senses, the here and now of worldly encounters. What Hurston gives us here, however, is an unsteady interplay of presence and absence, a gesture toward what remains invisible yet is somehow present and palpable still. We are led to glimpse, in Vincent Crapanzano's words, "horizons that extend from the insistent reality of the here and now into that optative space or time—the space-time—of the imaginary."[84]

What would it mean to be faithful to these images of another reality beyond the givenness of the here and now? What kind of empiricism could accommodate the presence—perhaps even the truth—of such spiritual beings and intangible forces? For what was at stake in the stories, myths, and visions that she related, Hurston insisted, was "life as we actually live it."[85]

Malinowski too was brought to the significance of myth by attending to the lived reality of the Trobriand Islanders. Take, for example, this passage from *Argonauts of the Western Pacific*, recounting the experience of coral atolls and lagoons for those who found each place to echo an event in the mythic past:

We must try to reconstruct the influence of myth upon this vast land-scape, as it colours it, gives it meaning, and transforms it into some-thing live and familiar. What was a mere rock, now becomes a person-ality; what was a speck on the horizon becomes a beacon, hallowed by romantic associations with heroes; a meaningless configuration of landscape acquires a significance, obscure no doubt, but full of intense emotion. Sailing with natives, especially with novices to the Kula, I often observed how deep was their interest in sections of landscape impregnated with legendary meaning, how the elder ones would point and explain, the younger ones would gaze and wonder, while the talk was full of mythological names.[86]

Such moments of wonder, Malinowski would later emphasize in *Myth in Primitive Psychology*, attested to the "living reality" of myth, the way that its tales and legends made possible the "narrative resurrection of a primeval reality" otherwise lost to consciousness and experience.[87] Myths could pro-voke unexpected ways of perceiving and interacting with the world at hand. Far from "an aimless outpouring of vain imaginings," Malinowski urged, myths were best understood as an active force in the myriad engagements of practical life.[88]

So be it with regard to the native mind and its primitive psychology. But what about those for whom these arguments were made so carefully? Myth and magic had a crucial role to play "wherever the elements of chance and accident . . . have a wide and extensive range," Malinowski wrote.[89] He also observed, at the same time, that the knowledge of a European fieldworker in such milieus depended on his own ability to keep "his powers of observation and his sense of reality under control."[90]

This distinction, the contrast between the credulous beliefs of others and the knowledge of those among us who have a more secure hold on reality, is a familiar one. And yet this well-known line is confounded once again by the way that Malinowski's fieldwork seems to have actually unfolded. What we find in his diaries and letters is an anthropologist constantly wrestling with visions, with unreal forms and phantom figures that disrupt whatever discipline and focus he can muster.

I felt too rotten to look and was bogged down in the trashy novel. Even in the fjord, where the sea was calmer, I could not manage to come back to reality.[91]

At moments, the pink silhouettes of the mountains appear through the mist, like phantoms of reality in the flood of blue, like the unfinished ideas of some youthful creative force.[92]

At night, a little tired, but not exhausted, I sang, to a Wagner melody, the words "Kiss my ass" to chase away *mulukwausi* [sorceresses]. I tried to separate from my companions, but they were apparently nervous, and the road was bad, too.[93]

E.R.M.['s] letters are considerably more subjective. I am transported— entirely, in a trance, drunk—the niggers don't exist. I don't even want to eat or drink.[94]

I tore my eyes from the book and I could hardly believe that here I was among neolithic savages, and that I was sitting here peacefully while terrible things were going on back there [in Europe].[95]

Such moments of drift and distraction, occasioned by the novels, letters, dreams, and figures that would come his way, do not have the consistency of a mythic corpus. And yet these instances suggest that the texture of the world as encountered by this fieldworker, the foreign reality given presence in his texts, is one shot through with invisible forces and ghostly presences, a here and now populated by the traces and remnants of many elsewheres.[96] In one of his letters to E.R.M. (Elsie Rosalind Masson, whom he would marry shortly after returning to Melbourne from the Trobriand Islands), Malinowski even writes of the fieldwork experience as inextricable from myth:

> I did feel a thrill to see all these niggers again, whom I used to see day after day and who then were quite familiar to me and not altogether devoid of attractiveness or repulsiveness. Then, they all suddenly ceased to exist and became a sort of myth in my working out of the material. And here they were again. It was this breaking of the unreal, this coming to life of a self-made myth, that gave me the keenest pleasure in my return to work and to Kiriwina.[97]

It is difficult now to read these words without a feeling of revulsion, not for the subjects of their description, but for their author. We have learned to see through the "mythos" of sincere and devoted fieldwork conjured by the European fathers of early anthropology, most famously by Malinowski.[98]

We have learned to question the idea that field experience makes possible a radical departure from familiar truths, discerning instead, in this very conceit, the play of occult forces of domination and racism, muddling our thinking with the phantom promise of radical alterity elsewhere. Here lies one of the most powerful lessons of anthropology's reflexive critiques of the 1980s and 1990s.

And yet, all the same, we might ask ourselves whether the drive to see through myth—whether the myths that others live by, or the myths we may propagate ourselves—enriches or impoverishes our grasp of the world at hand. Both Hurston and Malinowski show how mythic vision can reshape the realities we encounter as anthropologists and remake the texture of their experience. As Malinowski notes of shipwreck stories in *Argonauts of the Western Pacific*, "The fanciful elements are intertwined with the realities in such a manner, that it is difficult to make a distinction between what is mere mytho-poetic fiction and what is . . . drawn from actual experience."[99] Should we be seeking to tease apart such strands, or do we work instead with their knotted forms?

A book once meant to be called *Kula*, recast instead with a nod to the fables of Greco-Roman antiquity, *Argonauts* invites a feeling of kinship between the wonder that others may feel and the wonder that anthropology might itself provoke, as our own stories gain a mythic reach and consistency.[100] The question can be put pragmatically: what can an openness to mythic reality allow us to grasp in the world? What aspects of experience would remain otherwise unreachable?

THE CORAL GARDENS AND THEIR MAGIC, published in 1935 as the last of Malinowski's monographs set in the Trobriand Islands, begins with these words:

> This will largely be a study of human effort on tropical soil, of man's struggles to draw his sustenance from the earth in one part of the exotic world, in the Trobriand Islands off the east end of New Guinea. Nothing is perhaps more impressive to an ethnographer on his first pilgrimage to the field than the apparent futility of man's efforts to control it. This contrast is brought home with great force when, on your first voyage along the south coast of New Guinea or through the archipelagoes in the east, you are surveying almost at a glance the

character of this enormous expanse of tropical country. Chains of hills succeeding each other; deep transversal valleys which often afford a glimpse right into the heart of the country; the foreground, at times rising in an almost vertical wall of vegetation or again sloping down and extending into alluvial flats—all these reveal the strength of tropical jungle, the tenacity of lalang steppe, the impressive solidity of the undergrowth and tangled creepers. But to perceive man or even traces of him and his works you have to be a trained ethnographer. To the experienced eye the blot of withered vegetation on the waves of living green is a little village, with huts built of sere wicker work, thatched with bronzed palm-leaves, palisaded with dried timber. Here and there on the slope of a hill a geometrical patch, brown at harvest-time with the foliage of ripe vines or earlier in the year covered with the lighter green of sprouting crops, is a village plantation. If you are lucky you might even pass at night a constellation of smouldering fires where the bush has been cleared and the trees and brush are being burnt down.[101]

These elegant sentences compose a classic instance of "scene setting" in ethnography, a testament to the narrative significance of "being there," as Clifford Geertz has described it.[102] These words and the images they conjure, however, do something more than to establish the presence of an anthropologist in the midst of a field of study. There is also that other being who enters into this scene, someone invoked again and again throughout these opening paragraphs with a rhythm and repetition—"you would find everywhere . . . you could recognise at once . . . you would realise at first sight . . ."—that begins to feel incantatory.[103] Who is this "you," and whence the certitude of what this being will experience, in a place never encountered prior to these lines?

There is something profoundly strange about this mode of address, one that would seem to close, all at once, the gulfs of space and time that divide a reader from a world being read. Malinowski famously ascribed the "ethnographer's magic" to principles of field method that could yield "the true picture of tribal life."[104] The opening words of *Coral Gardens*, however, suggest that this magic, if we can call it that indeed, has as much to do with techniques of writing and persuasion in anthropology.

Magic, Malinowski argued, is an act of power, a practical means of attaining ends otherwise difficult to reach: the protection of a body from the ravages of disease, the securing of a canoe against forces of wind and sea, the growth of yams within the invisible depths of the earth. As with myth, the anthropological corpus on magic has always been shadowed by the problem of error, the question of how best to handle the impossible truths that magic proposes. This impasse between scientific and vernacular judgment, however, begins to dissolve once again if we pay closer attention to the manner in which knowledge takes shape in anthropology.

"Is not the man in white every bit as magical as the sorcerer?" Michael Taussig has asked, musing on the mystical potency of photographic images of Malinowski at work among his Trobriand informants, his color and bearing radiating the *mana* of magical force.[105] Indeed, this is precisely how the deeply metaphorical and imagistic language in Malinowski's writing would seem to work, operating like a magical spell, as a "verbal act by which a specific force is let loose."[106] The magical word, Malinowski wrote, intends something deeper than the communication of a message, aiming at a "verbal communion between the magician and the object addressed."[107] Is this not what this monograph's opening words seek, in closing the gulf between writer and reader?

At stake in the relationship between these two figures, writer and reader, are what the philosopher William James called "conjunctive relations," forms of interaction or continuity that ford the divide between disparate worlds, making it possible to conceive a common world of experience.[108] Such relations lay at the heart of the method James named "radical empiricism," a philosophy that would insist on the reality and efficacy of all that lies *between* what we tend to look for in pursuit of truth: discrete subjects and objects of empirical knowledge. Malinowski read James avidly in the early twentieth century, and he wrestled with the implications of his thinking for a philosophy of experience. In a sheaf of handwritten notes from 1919 on James and other philosophers, the anthropologist reflected on the alchemical powers of conjunction: "N[aive] E[xperience] contains not only objective elements of reality, but also subjective ones. They are not watertight. They interact with the intellectual elements of our consciousness."[109]

What Malinowski would later say about magic stands as an exemplary instance of such interaction. Magic, he wrote, could be understood as "the scene of action pervaded by influences and sympathetic affinities."[110] And its verbal spells rely on what he called "creative metaphor," recasting what was present as something more than here and now—"the word claims more than actually exists"—but then too, in so doing, working to bring that further reality into being.[111] *Imagine yourself suddenly set down . . .*

These may seem like far-fetched associations to make, between ethnographic writing and the practices of its credulous subjects. What, for example, of the stubborn intellectual hierarchies that would elevate scientific knowledge above magical techniques, distinctions that make possible the very enterprise of anthropology as scholarly pursuit? Perhaps the anthropologist was writing only figuratively when his field diaries recorded the "spell" that would come over him during his encounters with the fiction of Kipling and other writers.[112]

But then again, as Malinowski argued, magic is founded on the "belief that a word can grip the essence of things."[113] And here, "there is no science whose conceptual, hence verbal, outfit is not ultimately derived from the practical handling of matter."[114] There was no more than a "difference of degree," in other words, between the use of words in apparently savage traditions such as magic and the theoretical abstractions of modern science. Even now, as Malinowski would declare elsewhere, "'magic' seems to stir up in everyone some hidden mental forces, some lingering hopes in the miraculous, some dormant beliefs in man's mysterious possibilities. Witness to this is the power which the words *magic, spell, charm, to bewitch,* and *to enchant,* possess in poetry, where the inner value of words, the emotional forces which they still release, survive longest and are revealed most clearly."[115]

Consider what happens in Hurston's most acclaimed work, the 1937 novel *Their Eyes Were Watching God.* Crafted during a seven-week burst of writing in the midst of her fieldwork in Haiti, the novel delves into the life of Janie Crawford, a granddaughter of slavery who finds her way in the world through love and loss, acrimony and grief. So much of the story hinges on the capricious powers of language, on the force of "words walking without masters" through the ordinary milieus of black American life in the early twentieth century. Many of its events take place in Hurston's own Eatonville, where "big picture talkers" set themselves on the porch of the general store, "using a side of the world for a canvas."[116] Their raucous tales of bedraggled mules and philandering spouses gave shape to "crayon enlargements of life," the novel suggests, as if these storytellers "could hear and see more . . . than the whole county put together."[117]

Janie enjoys their banter in the years that she looks after the store, but then finds herself, on coming back to the town much later in life, the focus of cruel and vivid conjectures as to what she must have been doing in her time away. She dismisses these speculations. "'Course, talkin' don't amount tuh uh hill uh beans when yuh can't do nothin' else,'" she tells her closest friend in the town, Pheoby Watson. "'It's uh known fact, Pheoby, you got tuh go there to *know* there.'"[118]

Janie sounds like an anthropologist indeed when she insists on the value of firsthand knowledge. And yet, throughout *Their Eyes Were Watching God*, something else is happening that complicates this idea. For the entire novel unfolds as a story told one night by Janie to Pheoby, a recounting that takes the reader through all that she has seen and felt in the years that led to this moment of return: the dreams and desires of adolescence, the marriage to a brutal man that kept her in Eatonville for so much of her adulthood, the young lover she followed for a time of rekindled joy in the muck of the Everglades, the ferocious tumult of wind and water that would land her here once again, a bereaved widow once more. The book itself is a way of knowing there by going there, a story that bends the coordinates of time and space through the force of its telling. "The night time put on flesh and blackness," Hurston writes, describing what happens as Janie begins to speak the fullness of her life that night—"the kissing, young darkness became a monstropolous old thing while Janie talked."[119]

Pheoby is enchanted by what Janie says. "'Lawd!'" she exclaims. "'Ah done growed ten feet higher from jus' listenin' tuh you, Janie.'"[120] How are we to take these words of Janie Crawford's friend, Zora Neale Hurston's character, their metaphorical reach and their generative promise, so startlingly reminiscent of the spells for growing bodies that Malinowski had gathered in the Trobriands?[121] The world itself, Hurston tells us in *Mules and Men*, began with words of magical force: "Six days of magic spells and mighty words and the world with its elements above and below was made."[122] And this novel, *Their Eyes Were Watching God*, culminates with a metaphor that brings into focus the world-making powers of language itself. "She pulled in her horizon like a great fish-net," Hurston writes—"Pulled it from around the waist of the world and draped it over her shoulder. So much of life in its meshes."[123]

While these words concern Janie and the life that remains for her to follow, in the company of her stories and memories, they stand just as well as a testament to what can happen in the face of such writing. What else is this book, after all, than precisely such a fishnet, drawing within its perimeters the horizon of a world and the fullness of its life? Hurston's language reveals the generative powers at work in storytelling. We see with her books, as with anthropology itself, that these powers involve the conjuring of ideas by means of experience, through metaphors that ground understanding in the empirical substance of the world. Such figures mark the writerly way that anthropology thinks and works with the world at hand, through concrete images of life and embodied forms of abstraction. This is language mingled with the stuff of the world, bending its contours through the act of expression.[124]

"RESEARCH," ZORA NEALE HURSTON muses in *Dust Tracks on a Road*, "is a seeking that he who wishes may know the cosmic secrets of the world."[125] She recounts a time of searching that took her to the pine forests and mining colonies of Polk County in central Florida. There she finds herself in the company of fugitives holed up in turpentine camps, bleeding the trees for sap. She meets men "muscled like gods" on the railway lines, hammering spikes into steel for "the world must ride."[126] They belt out folk songs from ladders leaned against orange trees by day, she tells us, then over beat-up pianos and country liquor in the jooks each night. From the depths of the phosphate mines come shark teeth as wide as a workman's hand, ribs of ancient sea creatures spanning twenty feet in length. "Gazing on these relics," Hurston writes, "forty thousand years old and more, one visualizes the great surrender to chance and change when these creatures were rocked to sleep and slumber by the birth of land."[127]

The anthropologist sketches, with these impressions of fieldwork, the picture less of an *ethnos* than a *kosmos*, a world much bigger than the people and culture she seeks to know. Images of Florida come in the form of a litany, each framed by the repetition of a single place-name, "Polk County." And with every return to this toponym, what emerges is a different face of its reality, catching up its inhabitants in a riot of organic life, song, and explosive violence. The anthropologist too is caught up in these vicissitudes of fate, in the challenge of keeping pace with these rhythms of action and expression. Her first expedition to Florida, she admits, was so unsuccessful that what she'd gathered was "not enough to make a flea a waltzing jacket."[128] When she returns, she finds not only more, but fearfully too much. "It was in a sawmill jook in Polk County that I almost got cut to death," Hurston recalls.[129] Like the creatures disgorged by the phosphate mines, the fieldworker must reconcile herself to merciless "chance and change."

What does it mean to submit oneself to these vicissitudes, to seek out knowledge amid the clamor of the world? We could call it ethnography, as we tend to do with the methods of field research and writing we typically pursue in anthropology. But, given the span of forces and beings at stake in this endeavor, we might fall back instead on a term largely lost since the early twentieth century: cosmography, the record of a cosmos, the conjure of a universe other than our own.

Boas, Hurston's mentor, proposed the term as one picture of anthropological inquiry, in homage to the German Romantics Goethe and Alexander von Humboldt. "The cosmographer," Boas wrote, "holds to the phenomenon which is the object of his study . . . and lovingly tries to penetrate into its secrets until every feature is plain and clear."[130] There is more to anthropology, in other words, than the deduction of laws to govern the unruly proliferation of things and impressions. Our inquiries invite a devotion to the fullness of each object of study, a commitment to reveal each situation as a world unto itself, "worthy of being studied for its own sake."[131] Anthropology invites us to tarry within the depths of what lies at hand. And here is the true spirit of its empiricism, for the realities we seek begin within, but quickly spill beyond, the apparent certitudes of what is present.

"Empiricism is by no means a reaction against concepts, nor a simple appeal to lived experience," Gilles Deleuze writes in *Difference and Repetition*. "On the contrary, it undertakes the most insane creation of concepts ever seen or heard." What makes the generation of concepts through experience so "insane," for Deleuze, is that it mobilizes the power of "things in their free and wild state," taking the concept, that is, "as object of an encounter" rather than what we might attain if we move beyond the flux of life: "something in the world forces us to think."[132] He and other philosophers have reached for the idea of encounter to radicalize the empiricist tradition. This method, however, is already implied by how we work, in anthropology, with the conceptual richness of the world at hand. For the kind of thinking that anthropology nurtures begins with things of the world.

"To possess the sea and the stars and the universe—or at least to encompass them in one's thoughts?"[133] So Malinowski asked himself one evening on the island of Kiriwina, gripped with distaste at the mundane span of his ambitions. I do not think, in the years that followed, that he ever met Hurston in person. And yet I imagine that if he could have, through some confounding entanglement of time and space, and if by unlikely chance he would then have had the humility to speak aloud this vexation, she might have lent a measure of assurance to the novice European fieldworker with a promise like this one: "Just squat down awhile and after that things begin to happen."[134]

That sentence appears in a letter that Hurston penned to Henry Allen Moe of the Guggenheim Foundation in 1936. But the lesson is one that she may well have absorbed nearly a decade earlier while working with Cudjo Lewis or Oluale Kossula, abducted to Alabama from the West African coast on the last American slave ship in 1860. "When can I come again?" Hurston recalls asking him after one long Monday of conversation. "I send my grandson and letee you know, maybe tomorrow, maybe nexy week," Kossula replies.[135]

We don't know how long she waited for this next occasion. But we do know from *Barracoon*, the account that was published at last in 2018, that Hurston kept coming back over many days, for exchanges that arced between that Alabama porch and a life that spanned impossible distances. "Some days we ate great quantities of clingstone peaches and talked. Sometimes we ate watermelon and talked. Once it was a huge mess of steamed crabs. Sometimes we just ate. Sometimes we just talked. At other times neither was possible, he just chased me away."[136]

Such faith in the potential of what may come no doubt takes a unique kind of receptivity. Fieldwork asks one to wait with patience for the happenings of the world, and to find within them the seeds of thought.[137] These are singular and capricious encounters, these moments that compose the archive of our discipline. And yet, taken together, they yield a corpus of knowledge and experience, a body of learning we have come to call anthropology. So much turns, therefore, on how we learn to approach the palpable density of the world at hand. An encounter can recast the conditions of its unfolding, extend the horizons of that time and place. With care, and also with luck, experience may open into an unknown world of infinite depth and indefinite scope: a cosmic anthropology.

CHAPTER TWO

A Method
of Experience
Reading, Writing,
Teaching, Fieldwork

In 1982, the anthropologist E. Valentine Daniel applied for a research grant from the Social Science Research Council, hoping to study the folk songs of Tamil women laborers on the tea estates of his native Sri Lanka. By the time he arrived the next year, anti-Tamil riots had convulsed the country, his would-be singers desperately salvaging what they could from burnt-out homes. "Before I knew it, defying all research designs and disciplinary preparations," Daniel later wrote in *Charred Lullabies*, "I was entangled in a project that had me rather than I it." Straightforward words of research method like "evidence" and "informant" took on "terrifying meanings" among unrelenting tales of violence.[1] The anthropologist found he had no choice but to forgo his plans and to follow instead the trail of these rumors. Fieldwork became an effort to grasp the significance of an unexpected and fearsome circumstance.

A few years later, Gloria Goodwin Raheja—who had studied anthropology alongside Daniel at the University of Chicago in the 1970s—returned to a village in northern India that she knew well, to continue her own studies of caste and rural society. It so happened that she had taken her children with her, Raheja recalls in *Listen to the Heron's Words*. Her daughter staunchly refused to drink the water buffalo milk on hand, and so Raheja was forced to spend hours each day nursing the young child in the household courtyard. "I found myself sitting in the courtyard with her in my lap for a good part of the day, and so I turned my attention to the tapes," she writes, describing how she finally came to listen closely to the recordings of women's songs she had once made in the village. "The words of the songs . . . allowed me to hear, at last, that women were not the unquestioned bearers of 'tradition' I had assumed them to be."[2] Were it not for this accident of experience in the field, her book with Ann Grodzins Gold about women's expressive traditions in India would never have come into being.

We know it well, the character of the "anthropological picaresque," as Lawrence Cohen calls it in *No Aging in India*: "Something was wrong. I grew ever more desperate," so many of us, like Cohen, could say about our misadventures in fieldwork; "it was only when I abandoned *looking* for what I understood," for what I thought I knew, "that I began to find it."[3] I first read Daniel and Raheja in a seminar taught by Cohen at the University of California, Berkeley, in the late 1990s. And soon enough, I too would encounter the discipline's strange ways of eventually somehow working out, when my own plans for dissertation fieldwork in southern India went sour. How could I know whether it was in fact worthwhile, what I wound up pursuing instead in the name of research? "The mind is a monkey," a philosophical parable I often encountered in those years in India would warn. And yet I learned, like so many of my teachers and peers, that there was a way to reconcile oneself with the tugs of its curiosity, to let it wander a bit unleashed, to sustain the faith that something worth knowing would eventually be seen.

It is almost a truism and cliché to say that anthropology lands us in the midst of things unexpected. To dismiss this as a commonplace, however, is to leave opaque something essential in the generation and transmission of knowledge in the discipline. For what is at stake here is the relationship between truth and accident, the way that experience in anthropology invites us to stumble over insights of enduring value, as if the arbitrary and the abiding were somehow fused inextricably together in what we do. There is the deep uncertainty of the field environments in which we work, a "discordance" that demands, as Daniel writes, "a set of disparate and desperate forays into the roughest of waters in order to recover meaning."[4] There is also the challenge of bearing witness to this discordance in whatever we write and say thereafter, of carrying through this experience and its trouble. As *Charred Lullabies* reminds us, "The poesis of culture itself is a narcotic" and "Narcotics cannot still the tooth / That nibbles at the soul."[5]

Such are the difficulties faced by an intellectual enterprise that flits ever so restlessly between reportage and poetry, science and art. What does it mean for anthropology to be "the most scientific of the humanities, the most humanist of the sciences," as Eric Wolf once put it?[6] Think of all those methodological quirks that lend anthropology its peculiarity as a scholarly endeavor: pursuit of knowledge in unknown and often tumultuous circumstances; immersion in marginal and bygone ways of being in the world; the writerly traffic in metaphors, myths, and other deliberately affecting modes of narration; the inescapable presence of the scholar herself as witness and interpreter. It is undeniable indeed, to borrow from Clifford Geertz, the "oddity of constructing texts ostensibly scientific out of experiences broadly biographical."[7] And yet it seems we have no more and no less than precisely this, a method of experience.

THE QUESTION OF WHAT, if anything, makes for basic method in anthropology remains a vexed one. We may have come some way from what E. E. Evans-Pritchard reported in the 1930s:

> When I was a serious young student in London I thought I would try to get a few tips from experienced fieldworkers before setting out for Central Africa. I first sought advice from Westermarck. All I got from him was "don't converse with an informant for more than twenty minutes because if you aren't bored by that time he will be." Very good advice, even if somewhat inadequate. I sought instruction from Haddon, a man foremost in field-research. He told me that it was really all quite simple; one should always behave as a gentleman. Also very good advice. My teacher, Seligman, told me to take ten grains of quinine every night and to keep off women. The famous Egyptologist, Sir

Flinders Petrie, just told me not to bother about drinking dirty water as one soon became immune to it. Finally, I asked Malinowski and was told not to be a bloody fool.[8]

The discipline has become much more than an occasion for European men to expose themselves and others to the temptations and dangers of the feminine tropics, only to come home and coyly report on what might but certainly shouldn't have happened.[9] But as the identity of those who do anthropology multiplies; as the places they go diverge; as their topics of study and the forms of involvement they demand burgeon; as the tangible form of these findings proliferates, what holds all of this together as a coherent mode of inquiry remains a thorny problem.

Something in this difficulty has to do with the way that we are accustomed to thinking about method, as a matter of how-to advice or useful rules to follow. Taking up methods in this manner always raises the question of how to reconcile such abstract formulations with the concrete situations that they are expected to govern, a problem all the more severe in the case of anthropology, given the impossibly wide span of circumstances in which our research takes place. Say, however, that we approached the question of method as Lorraine Daston and Peter Galison do in their book *Objectivity*, as a matter of ethos as well as epistemology, anchored in quotidian habits of the knowing self. "The kinds of practices" that science involves, they note, "include training the senses in scientific observation, keeping lab notebooks, drawing specimens, habitually monitoring one's own beliefs and hypotheses, quieting the will, and channeling the attention."[10] Say we took a closer look at what happens when we do anthropology. What are the dispositions most crucial to our practice, the practical orientations that guide our work?

In anthropology, Victor Turner writes, "experience is a journey, a test . . . a ritual passage, an exposure to peril, and an exposure to fear," a form of "practical, yet poetical, knowledge."[11] Turner's words help to underscore that experience involves more than what happens in a given situation: there is also the question of how one is disposed to such happenings, whether they are taken as circumstances to be engaged or just endured. We know that fieldwork demands a spirit of openness to the unexpected, an attunement to its elusive promise as a basis for knowledge. Would it be so surprising if such an orientation, honed through intense trials undergone in some unfamiliar place, carried over into other milieus in which anthropologists also think and work? What dispositions toward the world does an anthropologist cultivate and carry between office and field site, library and classroom? Is there a consistency to what unfolds in the name of anthropology across these disparate domains? In what follows, I hope to trace the workings of a shared sensibility, the pursuit of experience as a matter of method in anthropology.

Recent years have seen forceful challenges to the idea of experience as a ground for knowledge. "Appeals to experience often act as validations for ethnographic authority," James Clifford argues in The Predicament of Culture, noting that classical ethnographies did more to convey the "personal knowledge of the field" gained by the anthropologist than the voices and viewpoints of their interlocutors.[12] In anthropology as with other disciplines in the humanities such as history and literature, experience has come to stand for a naïve ideology of individual identity, too closely tethered to the personal integrity of its subjects and exponents.[13] The phrase "my people" occurs in anthropology as a casual synonym for "my experience," Clifford writes.[14] And these days, such experience is all too susceptible to a market logic of exchange, the belief that worthwhile experience can be acquired and held like any other personal property.

Contemporary debates regarding the value of experience owe much to the way that the social sciences and humanities distinguished themselves from the natural sciences a century ago. Wilhelm Dilthey, the early twentieth-century German philosopher who made the most influential case for the value of Geisteswissenschaften, such as history, economics, politics, and literature, argued that these disciplines were uniquely concerned with the "self-knowledge" of living man: "we can only know ourselves thoroughly through understanding; but we cannot understand ourselves and others except by projecting what we have actually experienced into every expression of our own and others' lives."[15] Intellectual traffic in such experience has always been fraught with the risk of excessive emphasis on the unity and coherence of its subjects, a charge often leveled against Dilthey and other proponents of phenomenology. But then too, as Martin Jay notes with regard to these thinkers, "the subject of experience, rather than being a sovereign, narcissistic ego, is always dependent to a significant degree on the other—both human and natural—beyond his or her interiority." The idea of experience "involves a kind of surrender to or dependency on what it is not, a willingness to risk losing the safety of self-sufficiency."[16]

Far from something purely personal, then, experience may be understood as that which makes possible a break from the confines of an individual life, that which inaugurates a more fully implicated and even experimental mode of being. In English, the words "experience" and "experiment" have a long and intertwined history, attested by the importance of encounters with the unknown in various experimental practices, be they literary, scientific, or artistic in nature.[17] Experimentation in the natural sciences, Hans-Jorg Rheinberger has argued, involves work with scientific objects that embody "what one does not yet exactly know."[18] What gives anthropology its singular character as an experimental endeavor is the immersion of its subjects themselves in this field of uncertainty. Anthropological knowledge puts the being of its practitioners, readers, students, and interlocutors into question, subjecting all such experience to the torsions of foreign circumstance, to the vicissitudes of relation and communication, sensation and imagination. It is difficult to circumscribe limits to this movement, which seems designed to persist and pass over from domain to domain, one life into another.[19] Even an ethnographic text remains unfinished, Stephen Tyler says: "No, it is not a record of experience at all; it is the means of experience."[20]

With the idea of a method of experience in anthropology, therefore, I don't mean to imply that experience is our most essential object, what we seek most fundamentally to understand. I have in mind something other than a phenomenological anthropology that takes the travails of experience — "existential demands, constraints, dilemmas, potentialities, uncertainties," as Robert Desjarlais and Jason Throop have outlined them — as the objects of a particular domain of inquiry.[21] Instead, what I want to explore here is a different and perhaps broader idea, the possibility that what we do, when we pursue anthropology, is to put experience into motion as both means and end of investigation: to work *through* experience of a field of inquiry and work *on* the experience of those we share that inquiry with. For ultimately, as Eduardo Viveiros de Castro has observed, "the object and method of anthropology are versions of each other."[22]

In what follows, I consider experience as method in the work of four anthropologists: the structuralist and mythographer Claude Lévi-Strauss; the phenomenologist and writer Michael Jackson; the economic anthropologist of Africa Jane Guyer; and the scholar of science and ecology Natasha Myers. I rely, that is, on ethnographic exposure to four anthropologists at work, trying to grasp how experience matters in the making of anthropological knowledge. I focus on four kinds of ordinary activity essential to the doing of anthropology — reading, writing, teaching, and fieldwork — taking each of these in turn as a field of event and expression. These are disparate practices, no doubt, and I follow them in the company of men and women who hail from diverse intellectual traditions with French, Antipodean, British, and North American roots. Still, I hope to show that there are shared ways of working with the unexpected and its lessons: a unity of approach that might help to unravel what experience means for anthropology, and how one might think in times of fundamental uncertainty like ours.

THE WALLS WERE LINED with books, as one might expect. Among them were a number of wooden masks, woven baskets, and a tapestry of a bodhisattva. The desk was washed in light from the balcony window, over-looking the Rue des Marronniers in a gracious district of Paris. More than anything else, however, what struck me about the study where Claude Lévi-Strauss read and wrote for decades was the imposing door that regulated entry into the space. Built in several layers of white metal and wood, and spanning an astounding four to five inches in thickness, the door looked like something more appropriate for a bank vault than a personal library. Closed against the commotion of the outside world, the slab would reveal to the study's sole occupant a fraying and yellowed map of the languages spoken by the "Indian Tribes of North America," carefully buttoned into a protective plastic sleeve.

"I realized early on that I was a library man, not a fieldworker," Lévi-Strauss has said.[23] This distinction between field and study is an old one in anthropology, as we have seen. And yet the business of learning and engaging in the discipline could never be reduced to simply one or the other. Although recent years have seen the growth of multimodal forms of presentation in anthropology, such as films, podcasts, and art installations, written texts remain the most essential way to record and convey the lessons of the discipline. We encounter the history of anthropology as an archive of stories that assume their most enduring form in books, articles, and essays. And whether these texts are engaged aloud or in silence, whether in one's own company or in the midst of others, their reading is a sensory and embodied practice, as at home in the world and its myriad fields of activity as any technique of ethnographic immersion.[24] What does it mean to be absorbed in the anthropology that comes in the form of written texts? Does the practice of reading have anything in common with the field ventures we expect anthropologists to pursue?

Lévi-Strauss makes a uniquely compelling subject for such questions. His

Tristes Tropiques chronicles field expeditions undertaken among the Bororo, Caduveo, Nambikwara, and other native peoples of Brazil. But the structural mode of investigation that gained Lévi-Strauss renown grew from his meticulous readings of the evidence already gathered in the anthropological archive, as seen in the four monumental volumes of the *Mythologiques* that he published between 1964 and 1971. These efforts no doubt present a controversial legacy now for matters of experience in anthropology. "This sort of analysis presupposes a corpse," Victor Turner wrote, lamenting "an anthropology withering on the structuralist vine."[25] Take, though, as a counterpoint to this claim, these words from the "Finale" of the project: "Experience has taught me," Lévi-Strauss writes, "how impossible it is to grasp the spirit of a myth without steeping oneself in the complete versions, however diffuse they may be, and submitting to a slow process of incubation requiring hours, days, months—or sometimes even years—until one's thought, guided unconsciously by tiny details, succeeds in embracing the essential nature of the myth."[26] Doesn't it sound oddly like fieldwork, this practice of reading?

It was this question that led me to seek out Monique Lévi-Strauss at the Paris apartment she had shared with her husband until his death in 2009. The French anthropologist Frédéric Keck had worked closely here with

Lévi-Strauss on a recent edition of his works, and he kindly offered to take me back one afternoon in 2016 to meet Lévi-Strauss's widow. "He had his head full, he was afraid it would burst!" Monique Lévi-Strauss told me near the beginning of a long and spirited conversation, describing her husband's sense of a tenuous hold on the hundreds of Amerindian myths he had absorbed through a devoted reading of the ethnological corpus. She spoke of how this space in which we sat together, his former study, had been carefully soundproofed by Lévi-Strauss when they moved here in the 1950s: "He couldn't work with the maid singing while she was cleaning the windows, he couldn't stand all these things." And yet, she insisted all the same, Lévi-Strauss did his reading as an anthropologist, deeply immersed in the events of the world: whether encountering a text or the people on a bus, the very same attitude was at work.

"All of this was America, you see," Monique Lévi-Strauss said, gesturing toward one of the bookcases on the far wall. The books had been arranged here with geography in mind: works on North America on shelves above texts of South American ethnology, with Europe to the right and Africa below Europe. The massive wooden desk used by Lévi-Strauss was ringed by these shelves, and beside it was a cabinet full of notes on index cards that the anthropologist had made from his readings. Work with these cards would constantly take him back to the books, his wife recounted, leading him in a continuous movement between the desk, files, bookshelves, and typewriter. His swiveling armchair would turn so much, she told me, that it wore away the floorboards below. And indeed, when she lifted the carpet at that spot, I could see how these itineraries of reading and thinking had literally written themselves onto the surface of the floor, leaving behind the unmistakable impression of a circle in the wood. Everything in the study seemed to convey an idea of reading as a passage through space.

These reflections ought not to imply that what happened here was an aimless wandering. "My husband was a very meticulous, scrupulous man," Monique Lévi-Strauss insisted. Careful planning went into everything. Daily routines were followed precisely, deadlines met without fail. And yet, listening to what she said, it struck me that all of these efforts at control—including the massive door that bounded the study—were meant to ensure the fundamental openness that was thinking itself. For, as his wife recalled, what Lévi-Strauss sought from the books on his shelves was an experience of the unexpected. His index cards recorded individual sentences that had once stood out as significant in a particular text. But working with these cards, he would wonder what else was said in these works, beyond those words that he had extracted. "I want to go back to the book, and see what is really around," Monique Lévi-Strauss imagined him saying as he returned to those books. Surprise was structured into this practice of reading: the study was a disciplined space of undisciplined drift, a means of planning for unplanned encounters.

"I try to be the place through which the myths pass," Lévi-Strauss once explained about his method: "This operation is not the outcome of a premeditated plan: I am the intermediary through which the myths reconstruct themselves."[27] This process of reading and reflection, which Boris Wiseman describes as "the slow assimilation of the mythical material into Lévi-Strauss's own unconscious," also depended to a great degree on the experience of music.[28] The study, isolated so carefully from certain forms of ambient noise, was opened at the same time to the sounds broadcast by a radio that played as Lévi-Strauss worked, tuned always into Radio Classique or France Musique. "The words bothered him terribly," Monique Lévi-Strauss told me, explaining why he had preferred to listen to classical music while he read and wrote. The radio allowed for a "passive listening," she explained, releasing him from the more conscious and active engagement that selecting records would entail. As Lévi-Strauss himself would declare in *The Raw and the Cooked*, there was a fundamental affinity between music and myth: "The structure of myths can be revealed through a musical score."[29]

One of the most curious aspects of this book, composed as a series of melodic ventures—song, sonata, symphony, fugue—is the invitation to experience its passages musically. "When the reader has crossed the bounds of irritation and boredom and is moving away from the book," Lévi-Strauss writes hopefully in the "Overture" to this first volume of the *Mythologiques*, "he will find himself carried toward that music which is to be found in myth and which, in the complete versions, is preserved not only with its harmony and rhythm but also with that hidden significance that I have sought so laboriously to bring to light."[30] I have always been intrigued by this suggestion, which presents reading as a kind of listening. I thought of the reverence that Lévi-Strauss often expressed for the German composer Richard Wagner, from whose 1882 opera *Parsifal* the anthropologist once selected a line—"you see my son, here, time turns into space"—as "the most profound definition that anyone has ever offered for myth."[31] And so I decided to see what might happen if I devoted a week to read the book again very slowly, listening continuously to *Parsifal* all the while.

The Raw and the Cooked begins with a Bororo myth from central Brazil, the story of a young man trapped in a nest of macaws that Lévi-Strauss gleaned from the early twentieth-century works of the Silesian missionary Antonio Colbacchini. Picking out a series of concrete elements—feathers, waters, infection, incest—the anthropologist tracks patterns that wed this myth to others in a common field of transformations. Gradually broadening the scope of inquiry to encompass diverse tribes and themes, the book outlines a deeper level of systematic thinking at work in the myths, a logic of sensible qualities such as the titular contrast between raw and cooked states of matter. This is a logic best revealed, Lévi-Strauss argues, through a mode of analysis itself mythic by nature, a style of thinking that seeks "to conform to the requirements of that thought and to respect its rhythm."[32] Here is why the composer Wagner could be said to anticipate structural analysis in the form of his music. In *Parsifal*, Lévi-Strauss writes, "alternate images become simultaneous images, which are, however, diametrically opposed."[33]

Like all of the *Mythologiques*, *The Raw and the Cooked* can be difficult to read. Although I had staked out a place in my university library for a patient and leisurely reading of the book, I found it difficult to stay day by day with the dense texture of its allusions, its great digressive spirals of reflection. Lévi-Strauss himself acknowledged the risk "to lose one's bearings" amid the material he had gathered, and there was little solace in his assurance that "this may seem to be a roundabout procedure but it is in fact a shortcut."[34] Then there was the music I was also absorbing, many times over, on a pair of headphones. I'm no connoisseur of opera to begin with, and having read a fair amount of Nietzsche in college, Wagner was an enemy I had learned to loathe without ever hearing. The German libretto was opaque to me, as was the interplay of "pure diatonicism" and "chromatic flux" that critics have lauded in *Parsifal*.[35]

And yet, strangely enough, something unexpected happened during this peculiar mode of reading and listening. I was trying to keep my mind from wavering one afternoon as I read from a chapter on astronomy called "Double Inverted Canon." Then I noticed that I could anticipate, for the first time, what would come next in the hours-long flow of music and song that I'd been hearing now many times over. The harbinger seemed to be one sequence of four notes that came in and out of prominence at this point late in the first act of Wagner's opera. And once I'd noted this pattern, I could suddenly see that Lévi-Strauss also returned throughout this chapter to harbingers of another kind, signs of a coming rain in the form of constellations.

I saw that the chapter itself, like so much of the book, worked with myths whose existence the author had anticipated before identifying. Through an accident of convergence, in other words, the music brought into focus one of the fundamental ways in which *The Raw and the Cooked* was written, as a temporal structure of anticipation and recognition. I began to understand what Lévi-Strauss might have meant in suggesting that "the myth and the musical work are like conductors of an orchestra, whose audience becomes the silent performers."[36]

A text in anthropology gives its readers knowledge that retains a charge of the unknown, torquing always and ever through a familiar structure into an unexpected place. The experiments in reading conducted by Lévi-Strauss help us understand how this happens. Something may have taken place somewhere distant, something seen and reported, but the anthropological text does not resolve the significance of this occurrence for those who come across it. Instead, what we find in the discipline's literary experiments are "experiences made with writing and through writing" that unfold, as Vincent Debaene puts it, as "a true continuation of fieldwork."[37] To read a work of anthropology is to enter into a space of ongoing and open-ended encounter. What happens here might inspire boredom rather than conviction, a feeling of incomprehension rather than a sense of having a secure hold on something worth knowing. These uncertainties lend our texts their experiential depth and purchase. To read in anthropology is to kindle what Lévi-Strauss once described as "a neolithic kind of intelligence," one that "sometimes sets unexplored areas alight."[38]

WRITING IS A practice that has gained much more attention in recent years of anthropology than reading. Beginning in the 1980s, as we know well, writing took its place beside fieldwork as an essential dimension of work in the discipline. Think, for example, of James Clifford's pithy definition of anthropologists as "people who leave and write."[39] We have seen many critiques now of the conventions that govern ethnographic writing. Each year also brings new first-person accounts of the anthropologist as writer, and more good advice for aspirants wrestling with this most famously torturous task.[40] In the midst of these efforts, however, certain aspects in the experience of writing remain elusive and obscure. A writer can tell you how they have struggled and somehow managed to accomplish what they have done. But there is only so much that such retrospective reflections can convey regarding the nature of a process every bit as capricious as fieldwork itself.[41] Suppose, however, that we dove instead as ethnographers into the scene of writing as an active field of anthropological experience—this was the conceit that Michael Jackson proved generous enough to indulge.

Jackson is, without a doubt, the most prolific writer in contemporary anthropology, with literally dozens of works of ethnography, fiction, poetry, and criticism to his name. He is also someone who has penned a great many insightful reflections on the craft of writing over the years, as seen in a remarkable 2013 book, *The Other Shore: Essays on Writers and Writing.* "There are always two sides to every story," Jackson observes here: "the order we bring to the world confounded by the world's invasions of our most carefully cultivated spaces." A writer may find solace in the shape and coherence that her words bring to inchoate experience. And yet, Jackson also acknowledges, "it took me years to realize that writing must be allowed to come to us, like life itself, and not be hassled into answering our summons."[42]

I found myself wondering whether, as an ethnographer, I could capture something of the experience of this process as it unfolded, this interplay between an active striving and the painful necessity of waiting and acceptance. He and I began corresponding about the idea, and Jackson sent me the draft of an essay he'd been working on, called "Atonal Anthropology." Here too, I saw, the anthropologist offered tantalizing details of his experience as a writer: "I make myself available to thought, in the knowledge that my day's quota of words, insights, and images, will come to me unbidden, born of my dreams, of a walk in the woods, of a conversation with a friend, of a book I am reading, or in the course of cooking a meal or cleaning the house." How does writing emerge from such quotidian circumstances? How does one cultivate and prepare for something that would seem to happen so ineffably? With characteristic grace, Michael invited me to find out by spending a few days with him in Cambridge, Massachusetts.

I have no idea what will happen when I show up at his office door one frigid Wednesday in January. When he sees me, in fact, Michael confesses with a laugh that he hadn't been able to write at all that morning, knowing that I would be coming soon. He's been working on a novel, *Fathers and Sons*, and has now resigned himself to editing and revising for the remainder of the day. He settles me at a table facing his bookshelves before turning back to his desk and monitor. I try to make myself as quiet and unobtrusive as possible, listening rather than peering over his shoulder at the screen. Could I avoid being a distraction?

Remarkably, Michael is working with his door wide open, voices carrying from down the hall. I can hear how emphatically, even decisively, his fingers strike the computer keyboard. "It's the habit of hitting typewriter keys," Michael later explains. "I think of writing as a mechanical thing. I'm probably beating the shit out of it." As it happens, such habits and routines are essential to the practice of writing that Michael has developed over many years. He describes how he typically writes for no more than two hours of focused effort each morning, turning then to "all the usual chores of the academic day" before breaking in the afternoon to read, listen to music, or watch a documentary. Such things are also essential, Michael says, for they provoke the fragmentary notes and jottings that would propel his writing the following day.

We talk about these routines later that day on a walk around Walden Pond, close to his home in Lexington. "It's not as though nothing happens when you appear to be doing nothing," Michael tells me. As we pick our way along the slippery path, fishermen dropping lines through holes in the ice, Michael speaks of writing as both an act of will and an attunement to circumstance: "You just occupy the same space at the same time every day, and everything takes care of itself." How could he be so sanguine about this notoriously difficult task? Back at the house for dinner, I glance up at the trees leaning over the low-slung bungalow, recalling a struggle to prune these limbs described in *The Other Shore*. "Can we say that our minds are continually working" both consciously and unconsciously, Jackson muses here, "to organize our experience into forms that we can live with?"[3]

We take the road back to Cambridge the next morning under a sky still dull and orange. The cleaners are the only others around this early in the day at the Harvard Divinity School. On Michael's desk are books by Borges, Nietzsche, Achebe, Adorno, and Benjamin. At my table, I now have a monitor of my own that we've tethered to his computer, a device to see what is happening on his screen without having to loom menacingly over his shoulder. Michael didn't think this novel of his was something that I'd find interesting. But I've read enough of his work to know that his words would transgress the lines between ethnography and fiction, poetry and philosophy. And there is something riveting to me, as a writer myself, in seeing the words appear and disappear on the screen before me, in trying to follow the intricate movement of addition and subtraction, reversal and displacement through which these sentences gained shape and polish.

The scene being sketched takes place in a garage. There is a man, Mick, or perhaps his name is Jerry or Fergus, sorting through things heaped up over many years of life. I watch as Michael gives this scene thickness and detail, working between his word processor (a remarkably odd appellation, it should be said, as though the program alone were responsible for this process) and an online thesaurus. A sentence gradually takes form:

Certainly, Mick found solace in his trove, much as his son found pride in his library or a recluse might find comfort in his possessions.

Watching this line slowly emerge, I see how its ultimate form depends on the existence of many intermediate forms that finally disappear. Those three kindred adjectives, "solace," "pride," and "comfort," each hold a place in the sentence that had first been made by another word, "consolation," that eventually vanishes altogether from the page. It is as though this word, "consolation," placed and erased many times over, has served almost like scaffolding for the structure of the sentence, the framework of a possible expression.

"Every sentence has to have the right feel, the right weight, the right balance, the right length, the right words, the right combinations of sounds," Michael tells me later that morning, recounting the lessons of his early experience as a poet. His hands are cupped lightly as he speaks, as if he were hefting those imagined words, assaying their substance and quality. On the wall above Michael's desk is a framed painting beloved to him, Cézanne's

Large Pine and Red Earth. But the process of writing that he describes is more tactile than such visual art. "It's more like sculpture than painting," Michael says. "You take something off there and put it somewhere else. You're constantly working toward the point where the shape of the thing has those same formal properties of balance, weight, and feel."

On my final morning with Michael, I don't know what to expect. For him as for me, it is the week before the spring semester will begin, and there are many things he has to get done: email correspondence, a blurb to compose, letters of recommendation with urgent deadlines—in short, forms of writing essential to our trade and yet so unlike what I'd come here to glimpse. As he catches up on some of this work, I copy the title poem from his 1976 collection *Latitudes of Exile* into my notebook, admiring the image he had conjured of "paddling in the grey / shallow pools of our fixed phrases / like migratory birds / making a living here on the mudflats." Then, a few minutes later, and quite unexpectedly, Michael turns back to me. "I'm going to do a bit of writing. I don't know if you want to be in on it."

When I activate the monitor on my table, still tethered to the computer on his desk, I see that Michael has opened up the draft that he had sent me recently, that unfinished essay, "Atonal Anthropology." Beside the keyboard on his desk is a handwritten page of notes that Michael has made, listing various historical figures and the tensions running through their lives, stories that could help to show "how we are not all of a piece." These include, for Michael, the composer Wagner and the contradiction between his "sublime" music and his anti-Semitic rants; the tension between Heidegger's philosophy and his politics; the divided self revealed by Malinowski's fieldwork in the Trobriand Islands; and what Michael has gleaned from some of my own writings on the French anthropologist Louis Dumont in India. At the bottom of the page, Michael has briefly sketched parallels between the ambiguity of thinking and the ambiguity of being, the ambiguity of fieldwork and the ambiguity of writing, associations that gesture to the decades of sustained reflection that precede this moment. There are "oscillations between these modes of thought that are mixed," the anthropologist notes at the bottom of the page. How would these oscillations gain form and intelligibility in the writing now to come?

As I look on quietly, Michael begins to write about the unconscious immersion that unites various kinds of anthropological practice: "Doing fieldwork, writing an essay, or simply walking in the street, one may become so carried away by what one is doing that one 'forgets oneself,' and the lines between oneself and the other, or the task one is performing, become completely blurred." This in itself is an interesting idea to absorb with regard to the experience of writing. But there are always also moments, Michael adds, then clarifies in a subsequent paragraph, that bring us consciously and mindfully back to ourselves:

> This oscillation between experiencing oneself as one moment participating in and the next moment distanced from a social field or physical environment occurs both within consciousness *and* finds expression in behavior. My interest here, however, is in the alternative modalities of consciousness that I will call "being thought" and "thinking being." The first is a relatively passive mode of awareness in which thoughts come to me, or arise unbidden, as it were. By comparison, the second is active, because in this mode thinking is consciously engaged in, disciplined, decisive, and deliberative.

Michael often invokes this distinction between active and passive modes of awareness—it helps him make sense, for example, of what distinguishes scholarly writing from fiction: laying out an argument, say, rather than waiting for the right image or line of dialogue to strike. All the same, watching the writing of this highly analytical paragraph, I can see how the divide between an active thinking and a being thought is confounded by the very emergence of this text.

For the lines that snake down the page as the text develops keep circling back to what is already there, teasing out expressions of what can be thought from the body of words already present. The "thoughts come to me" are first identified, then later said to "arise unbidden." What begins as an effort to give in this paragraph a "compelling instance" of oscillation turns, with a lengthy and uncertain pause, into a more detailed discussion of the oscillation itself. Words like "both" surface and recede, only to surface once more. A "mode of awareness" is sketched at first as intrinsically passive, only to become "relatively" so, by comparison. Another mode seems to involve a sovereign figure—"I deliberate"—before slipping back into "deliberative thinking," the passive voice conveying that even this thinking is not autonomous, is still subject to a mode. Even the writer's own hands, in their momentum, overtake at times these words and ideas, reaching too far, pressing extra keys, y for u, u for i, forcing a halt for their removal.

Michael Jackson is an essayist, working most often in a genre that has long been likened to the experience of walking, a narrative mode taken even to involve "the perambulation of an idea."[44] This image of the essay form can help to convey what reading and writing share with fieldwork and other ways of being out and about in the world. But it may also suggest, perhaps, an overly integrated picture of the writer and their experience. The words I see develop, in my days with Michael, seem to explore the page and screen in a more decentered manner, pushing at once from many gaps and spaces in a movement that appears almost amoebic in manner. "In the act of writing, as in spirit possession, sexual ecstasy, or spiritual bliss, we are momentarily out of our minds," Michael writes in *The Other Shore*. "We shape-shift. We transgress the constancies of space, time, and personhood. We stretch the limits of what is humanly possible."[45] As I pay attention to his writing practice, I begin to understand what this passage might have meant, for the current of thought gaining form here has an agency that surpasses its thinker, ensuing in part from the matter of the words themselves, on the screen and on the page: the openings they make, the further associations they conjure.

Like the other kinds of transformative experience we know and pursue in anthropology, writing too begins in a field, a field whose forces, tendencies, beings, and things can shape in profound ways what we eventually express. The process of writing is a matter of acting in the world and being acted on by it, an accommodation to the circumstances in which we find ourselves and a way of putting these situations into palpable and intelligible terms. To say, as Michael Jackson does, that writing is an effort "to organize our experience into forms that we can live with" is to concede our own finitude as writers in the face of powers and matters beyond our capacity for mastery. For writing can still occur despite these limits, and may even occur more fluently with their acknowledgment. There is a value in learning how to declare, with the appearance of even a few scant lines of prose as Michael did that morning in Cambridge, these sworn words from *A Room with a View*: "Something tremendous has happened."

"THESE ARE GREAT systems of thought about fundamental questions, about what it's like to be human," she says. Jane Guyer, standing at the head of a small classroom in Gilman Hall, is lecturing about intellectual currents in postcolonial Africa. From where I'm wedged into a small space at the back of the classroom, I can see what she's competing with on the desktops of her twenty-odd undergraduate students: Facebook, Gmail, an online luxury resale store called The RealReal. Some are nodding off, while the more earnest ones speak of traveling to Africa, volunteering with a mission nongovernmental organization, research projects they're planning on AIDS and death rituals. "All the money in the world couldn't fix Africa," one student laments hearing from a friend. He fixes the professor with a pointed question— "Why does Africa need to be fixed?"

I am lucky enough to count Jane Guyer as a colleague in anthropology at Johns Hopkins University. At this research institution, as with many such places, there are professors who think of undergraduate teaching as a regrettable chore. Jane, though, is different, as I know from our conversations and from a semester of sitting in on her course, "Africa in the 21st Century." One afternoon, she appears in class with a bundle of Nigerian textiles, gathered and gifted over twenty years. She has a film to show on the "Mama Benzes" of West Africa, women who deal in African prints made and marketed from Europe, but there's a problem with the classroom DVD player. As one of the students wrestles with the machine, she takes the chance to introduce this lower-level class to prevailing habits of thought in anthropology. "We are always imagining that the world is going to surprise us," she tells the students— "always imagining that the world is going to knock on our heads and say 'Hello!'"

What she says seems important enough that I write it down twice—the second time, just to make up for the lazy and mostly indecipherable scrawl in my notebook. How she got here, I have trouble reconstructing. There was something she had said about Alexander Pope, about inheriting poetic and philosophical language, but, to be honest, I can't quite recall. I've been zoning out myself, absorbed in dissatisfactions concerning my own lecture class, which ended just minutes before Jane's, plotting ways of making amends onto the corner of my notebook page. Fitfully hunched over that sheet, I'm taken by surprise in what Jane says, which comes itself in the form of a knock—"Hello!"—a happening to make sense of retrospectively.

Instances of surprise, Guyer suggests in her 2013 Munro Lecture in Edinburgh, are moments in which "phenomena . . . declare *their own* existence."[46] At stake here, in other words, is the autonomous life of the unknown—a metaphor, perhaps indeed, but one that opens reflection on "the possible place of poetic imagination within an empiricist epistemology."[47] Borrowing a related image from the Nigerian writer Ben Okri, Guyer's lecture pursues the "quickening of the unknown" in anthropology, akin to the "mild fluttering feeling" characteristic of a certain stage of pregnancy,

the slight and nearly indecipherable movement of a "potential but as-yet unknown being."[48] Such inchoate forms of surprise demand sensitivity and attunement, Guyer writes: "The intuition and analogy of ordinary thought are
suspended, so that the phenomenon can be its own *form of life*, continuing
to make its own impression."[49]

How well do these reflections sit with Jane's advice to her class, with the
idea of being rapped on the head by some actual entity already afoot in the
world? Does the world knock, or does it flutter? Or, what kind of knocking is
this, that comes in the form of a fluttering movement rather than a knuckle's
hard ridges? I think about the forms that such knocking might take in the
space of a classroom like this one. The students' questions? Those Nigerian
textiles? The digital photographs on the pull-down screen? Guyer speaks
of the profound volatility of urban African environments, of corrugated tin
roofs wadded with paper to block the gusting sand. This room though is
such a quiet place, verging on the soporific as such places tend to do.

A few weeks later, deep into the semester, Guyer discusses mobile currencies in contemporary Africa. Small traders are reluctant to dispense with cash, she tells the class, given the spiritual, moral, and social dimensions of exchange, as well as the threat of hoaxing and other perceived dangers of electronic commerce—the scams, for example, perpetrated by Nigerian email entrepreneurs. "Do you remember Makoko?" Guyer asks the class, recalling the sawmills and intricate transactions of an informal settlement in Lagos they'd encountered weeks before. "Can you imagine them with mobile money? Can they manage all their deals with this?" Beside me, one of the students is online once again, but this time, at least, she's surfing a website for African news that Jane has encouraged them to consult.

Recounting a confounding episode of math education in Nigeria, Helen Verran describes the "disconcertment" of classroom experiences that reveal abstraction itself as an "amazing hoax of certainty."[50] Something in this spirit seems afoot whenever I drop in on Jane's class. It looks as though someone's always being asked to fiddle around with something, taking on a task that eventually proves more complicated than it should be: answering a question, getting a DVD to load, shouldering the discussion while the professor steps out to retrieve an object from her office. You get a sense of the unknown as something more than a vague idea; here, it's almost like a tangible form, a material artifact, shaped and honed as it passes from hand to hand, ever remaining unfinished. "If you're an artisan," Jane says, "you have to be attentive to the particular characteristics of the materials you're working with. Can they do this? Are they plastic? Are they fragmentary? Are they brittle? Are they the right color?"

I wonder, listening to Jane, whether she's thinking now of the minds of her students, shaped and molded by the able hands of their teacher—take, for example, that classic image from the depths of Western philosophy, the mind as a soft block of wax, stamped with the imprint of ideas and perceptions.[51] Receiving impressions is essential for Jane: "slow down, think, listen," she says, before adding one more thing—"configure it." An impression, in other words, the shape that an idea assumes, reflects a mutual accommodation between the knower and the unknown, in the way that artisans must bend themselves to the qualities of what they work on. "We're working through the material we've read together. I may know more than you, but I'm not an authority on it," Jane explains. This is what it means for the world to knock upon our heads: the material impresses itself on the teacher as much as her students.

The professor knows that there are students who have found her ways in the classroom frustrating and unsettling, who complain that her courses lack sufficient focus and organization, that they deviate, too unpredictably, from the dates and directions charted by syllabi. For Jane, however, such openness reflects a deliberate attunement to the life of the unknown, its potential to incite further reflection.[52] "Never be an authority on it," she tells me. "Teach it in the voice of interest. Look at this. I haven't got to the bottom of this either."

This paradoxical complicity between teaching and unknowing is what Jacques Rancière confronts in his reflections on the work of the eighteenth-century French pedagogue Joseph Jacotot. The controversial schoolteacher, as Rancière elaborates, sought to overturn the customary ideal of the instructor as one who "explicates" to others what they still don't know: "The master always keeps a piece of learning—that is to say, a piece of the student's ignorance—up his sleeve. I understood that, says the satisfied student. You think so, corrects the master. In fact, there's a difficulty here that I've been sparing you until now. We will explain it when we get to the corresponding lesson."[53] Jacotot's point was that the typical movement of mastery never ends: explication closes the gap between teacher and student, only to reopen it once again at a further point. True emancipation from this ceaseless regression of adequate knowledge, Rancière writes, is a task "that can only be performed by someone who effectively knows no more than the student, who has never made the voyage before him: the ignorant master."[54]

The approach is not without its hazards. The unknown delivered a literal knock to my head some years ago, when I tried to teach Kant's *Anthropology from a Pragmatic Point of View* to a class of Hopkins undergraduates. I had hardly read Kant at the time. Some feverish hours of cramming through the night lent precious little in the way of footing. I don't remember much of how that class unfolded. I think I may have posed a question about the faculty of understanding. Someone brought up space and time in the first *Critique*, which I hadn't yet read. I nodded gamely as the student went on about the place of the supersensible in the critical project, about which, again, I hardly knew anything at the time, losing myself in a state of inward panic. Everything began to go yellow, dotted with black, and then I found myself lying face-up on the floor with Jane Guyer's hand on mine. She, department chair that year, had already called for an ambulance to whisk me off to a nearby hospital.

Two days of tests yielded no more than a diagnosis of vasovagal syncope: simply put, I fainted in front of my class. Maybe from hunger, maybe exhaustion, maybe the weirdly swaying table in that classroom—or, maybe, the sheer vertiginous sense of not knowing where we were going, even as I was expected to lead them there. Back that Friday from the hospital, I saw that the provost had left a message on my answering machine at home—not an ideal circumstance, to be sure, for an untenured first-year professor! A few days later, one of the students wrote in with this report: "I don't know if anyone told you this, but after you blanked out for awhile, when you came to again, you actually repeated the last question you'd asked beforehand, something about abstraction—you were very persistent about getting an answer!"

I can't recall what that question was, or whether anyone had dared to answer the call of that woeful teacher darting in and out of consciousness. But Kant did have intriguing things to say in his *Anthropology* about abstraction and the unexpected. Surprise, "confusion at finding oneself in an unexpected situation," the philosopher observes, "at first impedes the natural play of thought and is therefore unpleasant."[55] Surprise bears such force on account of its affective nature, which suspends "the mind's composure" and "makes reflection impossible."[56] In the face of such experience, he writes, abstraction "demonstrates a freedom of the faculty of thought and the authority of the mind, in having the object of one's representations under one's control."[57] I can't help now but wonder: was I insisting then on abstraction in order to regain control of that classroom and the overly affective life of its thinking?

An apprenticeship in anthropology is a lesson in accommodating the unknown. We know this first and foremost from the vicissitudes of fieldwork. But is there any way of effectively teaching anthropology without surrendering ourselves to the force of surprise, in spite of its fearsome, and sometimes quite flattening potential? Think of the "method of wonder" in Marilyn Strathern's lectures, caught up in arresting involutions of the inside and outside.[58] Or of Hortense Powdermaker's reminiscences about learning anthropology at the London School of Economics, where Guyer herself first studied the discipline. "The lectures Malinowski gave in the classroom were not polished statements of a completed theory," Powdermaker writes. "He prepared them carefully—detailed charts and outlines on long yellow sheets of paper—but as he lectured, one could almost hear him continuing to think."[59]

What happens when the ordinary course of thought and action is suspended by something unassimilable? What is it to teach and learn in the midst of such moments? Take those familiar expressions of doubt that we associate with the problem of skepticism: how can I know, when my purchase on phenomena is so slippery and uncertain? The gravity of this problem depends on the kind of relationship we nurture with the unknown, on the shape and place that uncertainty assumes in our experience. "No method of inquiry yields infallible results," Jane Guyer writes, "but we nevertheless live in forward motion."[60] In the classroom as in the field, anthropology demands an openness to encounters with the unexpected, a disposition to the moment and its surprises, their unpredictable knocks and occasional gifts. "It is harder than it sounds," one student conceded at the end of that semester on Africa.

I PLACE MY HAND against the bark of the towering oak, trying to absorb something of the times it has seen: the lichens nestled into its crevices, the mark left by the foot of a stretching runner, the fumes from passing cars at this gateway into Toronto's High Park. It's never easy to prepare for fieldwork, which seems always to involve unforeseen challenges. Think of the vague and laconic advice that Evans-Pritchard famously dispensed: "bring a stool with you," and "don't get food on your fieldnotes," and "get interested in whatever interests the natives."[61] Figuring out what interests this particular native proves especially difficult, given its stolid arboreal presence. The woman beside me lays her face on the trunk, wraps its breadth in a warm embrace. I try to imagine, like her, what it must be like for the oak to inhabit this urban space—the strain of ripening acorns in the early summer, of living with this traffic and bustle.

My companion is Natasha Myers, an anthropologist at York, one of Canada's largest public universities. Her first book, *Rendering Life Molecular: Models, Modelers, and Excitable Matter*, has just won the Robert K. Merton Award from the American Sociological Association. The book describes the kinesthetic techniques and affective entanglements that enable lab scientists to model the crystallographic structure of proteins. Myers now is steeped in experience of a different kind, that of the oak savannah that took root here after the last Ice Age—in her words, "a 10,000-year-old happening." Trained first as a biologist and then in science studies, she approaches these plants as inquirers in their own right, as sentient beings feeling out a place through their physical form and chemical expression. She relies on methods of what Goethe called "exact sensorial imagination" to intuit what these dauntingly foreign beings are doing with their limbs and leaves.[62] And all of this is un-

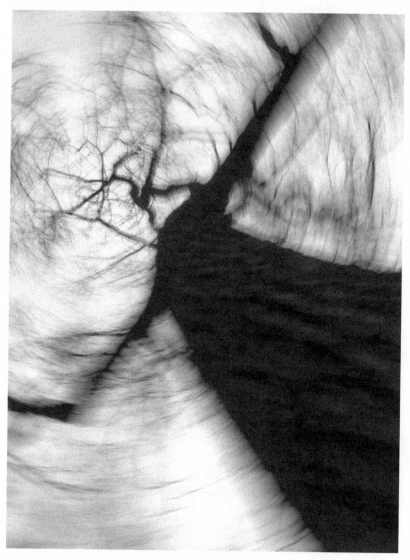

Dances with oak, 2017. Photograph: Natasha Myers.

folding in a 398-acre wooded park just down the street from where Myers lives in Toronto—a park close to where she grew up, a park where she sometimes ran and hid as a child. "I can't ever leave here," she tells me. "This work might take a hundred years."

Natasha has already been absorbed in this woodland's doings for many days over many months when I pay her a visit in July 2016. To follow her through High Park is to traverse a field of minor yet continuous events: a space of flaking wood once held by a log; the potent scent of a decaying bergamot flower; the blackened ooze leaking from the base of an oak; a pile of berry seeds heaped onto a winding branch. Unlike the lab environments she examined for her first book, this is a space shared with walkers, lovers, birders, mushroom collectors, soccer players, and countless other human enthusiasts. Some of the trails we walk along, Natasha tells me, date back to the many centuries of intensive use by First Nations peoples who shaped this landscape as an open savannah. Artifacts of that time can still be found here and there along the trails, and these histories of human occupation are essential to the story that she is crafting. There is also, though, a problem beyond the human domain that motivates her studies: "The space itself throws open questions. The space has stories it wants heard. My job is to become responsive enough, attentive enough, to sense or perceive them."

Birdcalls filter through the trees while we walk, as do occasional police sirens. We can't help but think about the reports that come each morning this week from the Republican National Convention in Cleveland, the politics of #blacklivesmatter, and the fallout from an attempted military coup in Turkey. Natasha hopes to find a way of speaking to such urgent concerns from the everyday evidence of life and death, growth and decay, in this urban ecological assemblage, a neocolonial landscape itself imperiled by modern regimes of management. Her attentions have been focused most closely on a two-acre area on the eastern edge of the park, a small space where she can recognize, remarkably, almost every individual plant we pass. For months now, she has been guiding "multisensory tours" through this area, inviting local residents to observe, sketch, hear, and imagine the living conditions of its vegetal life. Over a few days, I try out some of these exercises with Natasha, which she conceives as collaborative research protocols. She tells me to bend my nose to a goldenrod flower, asking what images it evokes. Struggling to put the elusive scent into words, I tell her it smells rich and sweet, like cold butter. Nearby, she has a pad and pencil in hand as she takes in the smell of a flowering Queen Anne's lace, drawing a sinuous line across the paper as a gestural diagram of its olfactory bouquet.

She abandoned a Ph.D. in molecular biology, Natasha tells me, because the genetic explanations she was taught to seek seemed too functionalist and simplistic. But when she encountered the problem of protein morphology, the difficulty of conceiving the intricate and dynamic shape of those complex molecules that give each cell its physical form, she found experimental practices completely at odds with the conventional picture of laboratory science. "It is the scientists who are caught," *Rendering Life Molecular* observes, describing the quirky ventures in calisthenics, mimicry, and dance through which crystallographers work out, with their own bodies, the most plausible physiques for these molecules: "modelers must learn to *move with and be moved by* the phenomena that they attempt to draw into view."[63] As we sit under the shade of one of her oaks now, Natasha recounts stories of scientists willing to be "made over" by the things of the world they seek to understand, a far cry from the idea of objectivity as a matter of distance and control. To me, what she describes sounds startlingly like ethnographic fieldwork, what she is doing out here in High Park, what I am doing with her.

Natasha laughs when I suggest this, describing a lab microscope advertisement she once found, portraying biologists as anthropological "seekers in the society of cells." Such efforts are still organized around the social and economic utility expected of scientific knowledge, she observes, while fieldwork in anthropology remains a more open and uncertain endeavor. "When you walk into a field, you can't say, 'I have my methods,'" Natasha elaborates. "You're going to have to experiment with how to pay attention, how to listen, how to tune in, whatever the field calls for." This spirit of responsiveness explains the unorthodox nature of the techniques she is developing here, such as the gestural diagrams that seek to render, in the movement of a line on paper, the fleeting trajectory of a floral scent. As we examine some of these drawings, which swoop and spiral like pollinators through the pages of her notebook, Natasha describes them as field notes of a kinesthetic kind, tracings meant to intuit and record a full-bodied experience of this place. For what is at stake here are not things in themselves but things as they take shape in an encounter. "I'm the instrument," she explains. "Changes in me also matter. Changes in the plant, changes in how I perceive the plant, all of this is data."

In a 2012 essay, she calls it "involutionary momentum," the way that an observer can be tugged into intimate closeness with the life of other organisms, as with the strikingly delicate and even sensual drawings of orchid-wasp relationships made by nineteenth-century naturalists such as Charles Darwin.[64] As a feminist anthropologist of science, she hopes to build on such neglected legacies in the history of scientific practice, in order to "keep open what it is possible to see, say, feel, imagine, and know about the stuff of life today."[65] One evening in Toronto, I tag along back into the park with Natasha and one of her collaborators, the filmmaker Ayelen Liberona. Both women are trained in dance, and they have been experimenting with movements that convey how grasses, shrubs, and trees bend with wind and grow into the light. This too is a matter of attunement, a way of approaching how vegetal beings understand their environment.

"Our morphological imagination is so plastic," Natasha says, describing how these experiments are meant to approach the sensorium of the plants themselves, the rhythms and sensations that shape their perception of this landscape. Here too, as ever, that essential aim of ethnographic fieldwork remains: allowing our mode of knowing to be remade by other ways of knowing.

Pondering this challenge with Natasha and Ayelen, something also happens to me. As I try to imagine, with them, the woodland around us as an active field of inquiry rather than a passive object of knowledge, everything begins to look like a medium of expression, maybe even communication: the hollow burl at the base of a tree, the deep holes dug into the forest floor by dogs. Curious, I wonder what it would be like to speak to Natasha from one of these holes, from the perspective of a plant looking up from the soil. The two of them laugh as my head disappears into the ground, our voices reaching each other now as muffled vibrations through the earth. Lying flat on my back, head within a hollow, I can feel and even smell this earth as we converse, for their voices are conducted by tendrils of roots, which release, with each word or sound, fine particles of silt onto my face.

"You did fieldwork!" Natasha exclaims when I emerge a few minutes later, acephalous anthropologist, body encrusted with leaves and dirt. It turns out that the nascent field of plant neurobiology locates the minds of plants in their root systems.[66] And we have stumbled together on an unexpected way of confronting an abiding problem in Natasha's research: how to converse with sentient beings that don't have heads like ours.

The "schooling of the senses" in science, Daston observes, involves learning to see a common world otherwise, to perceive uncommon facts in an ordinary world.[67] The truths that anthropologists seek, the conditions in which we work, and the ways that we communicate our findings may indeed magnify such estrangement. Let us not neglect, though, what can also happen to our being as we pass through this process. For it is difficult to say that anthropology concerns the experience of someone else or somewhere else in particular, whether a human society or a community of animals and plants. To be sure, our ventures often begin this way. But rarely do they remain as such, for everything turns on the extent to which the anthropologist herself becomes a vector of transmission, a medium to take in and pass onward the force of a transformative encounter. Observer and observed commingle and work on each other to the point where neither remains as they once were. The subject of experience in anthropology is neither self nor other but the open and dynamic field of their encounter—experience, in other words, not of whom, but of what.

IT HAS LONG BEEN a dictum of anthropology that its methods cannot be taught, only undergone. "The style, set early in the century, of giving a student a good theoretical orientation and then sending him off to live among a primitive people with the expectation that he would work everything out for himself survives to this day," Margaret Mead observes in her 1972 memoir, *Blackberry Winter*. "Men who are now professors teach their students as their professors taught them, and if young fieldworkers do not give up in despair, go mad, ruin their health, or die, they do, after a fashion, become anthropologists."[68] These risks are serious, the physical and existential trials endured by these scholars in circumstances beyond their control.[69] In a field whose research often takes women scholars in and out of disparate domains of male authority, instances of sexual harassment and gender violence are far from uncommon.[70] And episodes of misery, loneliness, tedium, and radical doubt are almost inevitable.

Preparation for such challenges can be a maddening conceit. One may be taught the value of in-depth conversations, copious notes, and sustained exposure to a novel place. But as Renato Rosaldo learned in the highlands of the Philippines in 1981, work in anthropology can suddenly throw one into moments of unthinkable force:

I stare at the fly.
One back leg rubs
the other.

Sky and earth heave,
press together.

Pressure
on my lungs,
tidal welling

overwhelms
my exhalation.[71]

Rosaldo and his partner, Michelle Zimbalist Rosaldo, had just arrived in Ifugao for two months of fieldwork when she slipped from a narrow cliff-side trail and fell to her death in the river below. Renato, looking after their two young children in the village at the time, was crushed by the sight when her body was found. "I began to fathom the force of what Ilongots had been telling me about their losses through the accident of my own devastating loss and not through any systematic preparation for field research," he later wrote.[72]

Decades later, he would recount the event in an extraordinary book of poetry, *The Day of Shelly's Death*. Poems such as "The Fly," above, do not try to draw lessons from this death in any straightforward way, as if to turn this moment of incomparable grief into a resource for generalization. And yet there is a different kind of teaching that these words countenance, a task more ethical than technical, asking their readers to imagine being given over completely to the sheer evanescence of life. "The work of poetry, as I practice it in this collection, is to bring its subject—whether pain, sorrow, shock, or joy—home to the reader," Rosaldo writes. "It is a place to dwell and savor more than a space for quick assessment."[73]

Acknowledging the text itself as such a difficult place to dwell stretches our sense of what is a field and where it may be found in anthropology. "Fieldwork," Akhil Gupta and James Ferguson write, "may be understood as a form of motivated and stylized dislocation."[74] Given what we have seen here in the company of anthropologists at work, we might ask what conditions and circumstances allow for such displacement. For when we look across the range of those practices most essential to the discipline, what we find is that they have a surprising amount in common with each other. Reading or teaching, encountering others or writing about these encounters, ensconced in a study or out and about in a wider world: could the difference between these activities and their places be a matter of degree rather than a matter of kind?

At stake here is the very sense of "the field" in anthropology. "Our fields of experience have no more definite boundaries than have our fields of view," William James suggests. "Both are fringed forever by a *more* that continuously develops, and that continuously supersedes them as life proceeds."[75] The field of anthropology may be found wherever we are in the company of someone or something that focuses and kindles this "more," that pushes us beyond ourselves in novel and unexpected ways. "Being there," somewhere else, does indeed matter, whether on a boat or through a book, whether caught in the twists of an unfinished sentence or captivated by the charge of a classroom tale. We ought not to think of this, however, as something to sally forth to, only then to return home, of stumbling, that is, on profoundly unsettling things before submitting those encounters to a necessary domestication. This idea of the field as a break or hiatus obscures what is most crucial about the experience, its transformative power, which must be carried over somehow, across the divide between places familiar and strange.

"An experience has a unity that gives it its name," John Dewey writes. "The existence of this unity is constituted by a single *quality* that pervades the entire experience in spite of the variation of its constituent parts."[76] Qualitative unity is what we find among the reading, writing, teaching, and research of anthropology: a force of encounter that passes onward across these distinctive domains, that carries the metamorphic charge of the unknown through diverse mediums of expression. Such is the *method* of experience unique to anthropology: working through experience of a field and working on the experience of those we share it with, a collective passage into altered states of being and understanding that can be focused and honed in consonant ways by all the various techniques at our disposal. To be sure, knowledge always relies on experience in one way or another. What distinguishes anthropology is this unity of process and endpoint, method and object, means and ends. This is the source of the discipline's singular frustration and exhilaration, the sense of being caught in a movement that doesn't let up.

Consider what we see of an anthropologist's life in Michael Jackson's candid memoir, *The Accidental Anthropologist*. We follow him through years of fieldwork in West Africa and the Australian outback, times of penury survived through proofreading and construction work, a blowout party in the department office at the University of Auckland that saddles young Michael with the reputation of a firebug, and a moment decades beyond his Ph.D. when he is forced to work as a dishwasher at the Australian National University in Canberra because the department there doubted whether he was truly "committed" to anthropology.

Jackson admits ambivalence at the prospect, shortly thereafter, of a professorial job in Bloomington, Indiana, even after years of fitful and irregular employment. "Despite the hardships of life on the edge," he writes, "my hands, like the hands of Sisyphus, were pressed against the gritty surface of reality, and I did not want to lose this sensation of the weight of the world."[77] This feeling for Jackson is far more than an idle conceit, attesting instead to a deep intimacy between knowledge and experience in anthropological practice. For our understanding, he observes, "is the outcome of an experiment in which one risks oneself," insight born of the effort to grasp, in the company of others and amid the tumult of circumstance, "the extent to which a socially conditioned human being can become other than he or she is."[78]

These risks take on an especially challenging valence in circumstances such as we have them now in American anthropology, where tenuous career prospects and precarious terms of employment have become the baseline for advanced training in the field. In one among many powerful reflections on these conditions, Jennifer Carlson, a recent Ph.D., warns of "how we may romanticize contingency's potential for noble suffering or heroic subversion."[79] The concern is a serious one, and some may see this essay as having fallen prey to this danger. What I have tried to show, though, is that contingency in a broader sense has long been essential to the practice of anthropology. And if this is the case, it is all the more essential that we find ways of ensuring that these processes of learning and doing can unfold under conditions of requisite freedom and care. For what is at stake here is the possibility of a "limit-experience" as Michel Foucault described it, "aimed at pulling myself free of myself, at preventing me from being the same."[80]

The prospect of such transformation seems ever on the horizon with anthropology, an endeavor that verges on the ethical and even spiritual, one that undoes the distinction between intellectual and practical life. In this work with the unexpected and its lessons, we confront the challenge of engaging creatively with the recalcitrance of a wider world, and folding such responsiveness into the tissue of our understanding. Whether we deal with strangers or friends, living faces or machine interfaces, humans or plants or even stones, such is the promise of experience in this field.[81] Anthropology is a practice of metamorphic passage, a deflection of thought through the vicissitudes of life.

CHAPTER THREE

For the Humanity Yet to Come

Politics, Art, Fiction, Ethnography

This is a peculiar time for *anthropos*, that living being at the heart of our inquiries in anthropology. Many have come to think of our time as the culmination of an "Anthropocene," an era of human planetary dominion, with more land, water, and biological life seized for our wants and wastes than ever before. At the same time, the unprecedented scale of economic inequality and racial violence in many countries, and acute refugee crises around the world, reminds us of the precarious and vulnerable conditions in which so many people must eke out a living. As the idea gains credence that our very dominion might be our undoing as a species, the question of how to reimagine what it means to be human appears more pressing than ever. "The Anthropocene brings the human back with a vengeance," Bruno Latour observed in his 2014 address to the American Anthropological Association.[1]

Anthropologists now find themselves in the midst of countless efforts to grasp the nature of humanity as a whole.

"Climate change," Dipesh Chakrabarty writes, "poses for us a question of a human collectivity, an us, pointing to a figure of the universal that escapes our capacity to experience the world."[2] We may be inclined, in the face of such figures, to insist on the significance of position and particularity, to draw distinctions between those most responsible for such calamities and others who may be far more susceptible to their consequences.[3] Still, we ought not to neglect that other side of anthropological reasoning, the abiding endeavor to wrestle with the human as such, with humanity as an object of reflection and imagination far beyond the scope of any concrete experience. Arguably, this has always been the moral and political ground of the discipline itself: an unsettling of what we take for granted regarding the human, through the glimpse of a horizon beyond. Anthropology began as a comparative enterprise spanning far-flung settings—we are familiar with troubles of this scale.

One of the most intriguing and provocative ways that the discipline has begun to wrestle with the ecological impasses of the present is through the pursuit of ethnography in the company of species other than our own. As Eben Kirksey and Stefan Helmreich ask in their introduction to an influential 2010 special issue of *Cultural Anthropology* on this topic, "What happens when *Homo sapiens* and its interspecies, multispecies, and quasi-species familiars, burrow into the biology that animates anthropos?"[4] Anthropologists have turned for insight and even solace to the ways that human lives are bound up with diverse communities of animals, plants, microbes, and other organisms. By paying attention to such "more-than-human socialities," Anna Tsing suggests, "we might get to know other-than-human worlds in which we participate, but in which we don't make the rules."[5] Such efforts aim to confound the idea of human being as somehow unique and exceptional, by insisting on its entanglement with other living beings. As Dorion Sagan observes, "We are crisscrossed and cohabited by stranger beings, intimate visitors who affect our behavior, appreciate our warmth, and are in no rush to leave."[6]

At stake in these arguments is what one might call the ontology of human being: how we conceive the substance of the human, whether we attribute any singularity to it, and how we understand its capacities for transformation. For if there is anything that the Anthropocene demands from its human protagonists, it is change in how they are and what they do. In the

Western intellectual traditions that anthropology seeks to trouble, it has long been argued that the dynamism of human beings depends on the transcendence of a natural world beyond the human, the overcoming of an animal nature and its moral shortcomings. Multispecies ethnographies rightly question this idea, insisting on the creative force of interactions and entanglements with diverse kinds. But we may also ask whether, in our keenness to excavate these relationships, to take "anthropology beyond humanity," as Tim Ingold suggests, or "anthropology beyond the human," as Eduardo Kohn has argued, we are neglecting how the human moves beyond itself.

Take Kohn's book *How Forests Think*, one of the most inspiring of recent efforts in this vein. "An anthropology that focuses on the relations we humans have with nonhuman beings forces us to step beyond the human," Kohn argues.[7] His book introduces us to a living world that is communicative through and through, a forest milieu teeming with diverse beings that think through images and tactile signs, that catch up its human inhabitants in broader webs of value and significance. "They force us to find new ways to listen," Kohn writes. "They force us to think beyond our moral worlds in ways that can help us imagine and realize more just and better worlds."[8] Transformation of the human is indeed at stake here. But this is change propelled from beyond its proper domain, from somewhere other than those things that Kohn understands as exclusively human: morality, language, culture. "The symbolic," he writes, "is something that is (on this planet) unique to humans."[9] For these humans to find a way to live more responsibly, on this planet, they would need to acknowledge their coexistence with other creatures that strive, speak, and share a life in profoundly different ways.

The ethical task that Kohn outlines is timely and compelling. I worry, however, that like some other ventures in the anthropology of nonhuman entanglements, his efforts in his book fall back too quickly on a certain picture of what the human *is*, beyond these entanglements. The significance of what happens in moral, expressive, and cultural life lies precisely in its promise to sustain creative activity beyond the limits of any given mode of being. Moral reflection and practices of cultivation; possession by ritual mantras or a profoundly good story; the forging of new understandings as the foundation of a life led in common: these are forms of experience that put the field of the human into play, that make possible the project of becoming some other kind of being. Furthermore, study of such movements in human life is what allows anthropology to conceive humanity in radically contrary terms. These dimensions of experience have long been essential resources in anthropology's engagement with ethical and political matters.

"The discipline is tinged from the root by the subjunctive mood," Michael Carrithers writes, describing the sense of moral possibility that defines anthropology: "Given the unity of humankind and the evident malleability of our species, anyone *could have* been someone else, those in any one sociocultural order *could have* participated in any other."[10] The challenge we face now lies in whether and how this sense of possibility can be expressed in a more expansive fashion, accommodating a feeling of kinship and affinity with diverse beings more deeply unlike ourselves, in coming to see, as Donna Haraway writes, "that all earthlings are kin in the deepest sense."[11] And in this endeavor, anthropology has a crucial method to contribute: its fundamental mode of imagination, its approach to humanity as an open horizon of displacement rather than a fixed position in the world.[12]

How should anthropology respond to the Anthropocene, to this picture of a planet at the mercy of human obduracy writ large? We can learn to approach this problem, I would argue, by doing what we long have done: by working to nurture a humanity yet to come.

WITHOUT A DOUBT, the idea of humanity has always been a vexed one. "Humanity is a difficult—sometimes dangerous—category," Ilana Feldman and Miriam Ticktin write. "Its promise of universal connection is also its peril of imperial expansion. Its capacity to evoke compassion for others is matched by its tendency to identify these others as threats."[13] These complexities arise in part because humanity is a term both descriptive and prescriptive, identifying a population of human beings, on the one hand, but also a desirable moral state ideally associated with those beings, on the other. There is also the fact that, as a category, humanity brings into play both abstract ideas and concrete practices of intervention. Take the charged domain of global humanitarian politics, which, as Didier Fassin argues, "is founded on an inequality of lives and hierarchies of humanity."[14] A sense of responsibility may propel incursions into the lives of others in the name of a common humanity. But as Fassin shows, this often implies tacitly that the lives of those who intervene are superior in value to the lives of those they seek to treat or protect.

One of the most profound and enduring hierarchies expressed in the idea of humanity is one that elevates the human above the animal, and, by extension, above the whole of nature beyond the human. A powerful critique of such dualism is found in Philippe Descola's important book *Beyond Nature and Culture*. The problem lies in what he calls the "modern naturalist ontology," the idea that in Western thought, humanity and nature are autonomous domains, fundamentally independent of each other.[15] "Dissident voices" have occasionally objected, Descola acknowledges, but this binary grammar, he argues, remains essential to various ways of affirming the human.[16] Even anthropology "takes our reality for granted as a universal fact of experience" by insisting on the value of cultural diversity, a commitment that seems always to betray an implicit faith in the underlying unity of nature.[17] "Anthropology is thus faced with a daunting challenge," Descola writes: "either to disappear as an exhausted form of humanism or else to transform itself by rethinking its domain and its tools in such a way as to include in its object far more than the *anthropos*."[18]

Essential resources in this task, for Descola, arise from alternative schemas for human relationships with the world—the animism of Amerindian thought, for example, which concerns "not Man as a species but humanity as a condition" shared by all living beings.[19] Yet, I would argue, if we turn our attention from this time of apparent senescence in Western humanism, back to some of its founding moments, certain other possibilities surface that we ought not to neglect or foreclose. I have in mind the eighteenth-century German Enlightenment philosopher Johann Gottfried Herder, whose work, intellectual historians have shown, was deeply consequential for the very emergence of anthropology as a field of inquiry.[20]

Herder pursued what he called a "natural history of humanity," one that accepted that "nature developed the form of the *human type* as manifoldly as her workshop required and allowed."[21] Without a doubt, Herder understood humans as exceptional beings, uniquely gifted with language and reason. Still, these gifts emerged and developed in continuity with dynamic forces of nature, rather than in dualistic opposition, "from rocks to crystals, from crystals to metals, from metals to the world of plants, from plants to animals and finally to man."[22] The "naturalism" in Herder's thinking, as John Zammito explains, engaged a "fertile and unpredictable creativity in Nature, and a . . . notion of fundamental forces which could encompass even the emergent properties of human consciousness."[23] Here lies another way of approaching humanity as both object of thought and moral ideal, a mode of being that developed out of nature yet remained open to its generative powers.

For Herder, the *Humanität* of humans lay in their capacity for sympathizing with the condition of beings unlike themselves; as he wrote in his *Outlines of a Philosophy of the History of Man*, "nature has formed man most of all living creatures for participating in the fate of others."[24] This feeling of sympathy could be provoked by the sound of someone suffering, or the sight of a dead friend, but, crucially, it relied on a sense of likeness that could extend far beyond the boundary of the human as such. "There are men who cannot bear to see a young green tree cut down or destroyed," Herder wrote; "a feeling man views not the writhing of a bruised worm with indifference."[25] For the eighteenth-century philosopher, this profoundly open sense of kinship—with "the morning star and the little cloud beside it," between "you and the worm that you are now squashing"—was a moral sensibility that could be cultured and cultivated.[26] "Feel yourself into everything," Herder exhorted readers; indeed, as Sonia Sikka has argued, his detailed accounts of Asian, African, and other far-flung peoples "have as their motive an expansion of imagination that would allow the reader to see the humanity of these various peoples, precisely through an understanding of the culture in which that humanity is expressed."[27]

What do we make of these portraits that Herder sketched based on the European travel literature of his era, descriptions that land at times on the "diminutive, ugly" inhabitants of Tierra del Fuego who "lack solid houses as well as warming fire," or the "Negroes" of Africa, whose bodies seem "formed, even to the nose and skin, for sensual animal enjoyment"?[28] Such judgments would seem to support the idea of Enlightenment philosophy as a handmaiden to European imperialism, the widespread sense that diverse strands of Western thought—including anthropology and ethnology—justified colonial conquest by distinguishing between superior and inferior peoples. We ought to recall, however, that for Herder humanity had no "prototype" in any one culture or civilization: "Let one have no pet tribe, no favorite people on the earth," he insisted.[29] Colonialism was contemptible precisely because it denied the humanity of others, and it arrested their efforts to develop that humanity on their own terms.[30] "Our part of the world must be called," Herder wrote in his *Letters for the Advancement of Humanity*, "not the wise, but the *presumptuous, pushing, tricking* part of the earth; it has not cultivated but has destroyed the shoots of peoples' own cultures wherever and however it could."[31]

As this observation may suggest, the eighteenth-century philosopher was an influential proponent of what we know now as cultural relativism. It is crucial to try to grasp, however, what this controversial idea might have meant for Herder. To speak of many cultures, nations, or peoples did not imply that there was a single and uniform nature that formed the backdrop for their cultural diversity.[32] Instead, Herder wrote of various environments of "living creation," each a "great garden in which peoples grew up like plants, to which they belong, in which everything—air, earth, water, sun, light, even the caterpillar that creeps upon them and the worm that consumes them—belongs to them."[33] These were dynamic forms of collective life, rather than fixed entities, each culturing, cultivating, or developing some specific form of humanity.

Rather than evacuating the possibility of moral judgment in the face of such diversity, in other words, which relativism is often taken to do, Herder's embrace of difference demanded a moral commitment to the ethical value of such *Bildung*, or cultural formation.[34] "The mind nobly expands," Herder wrote, "when it is able to emerge from the narrow circle which climate and education have drawn round it, and learns from other nations at least what may be dispensed with by man."[35] Such education in humanity, as both a moral task and a method of inquiry, would prove a crucial legacy for the emerging field of anthropology.

With his reflections on what "a penetratingly perceptive human being" could learn among foreign peoples by observing the circumstances of their lives and "participating in their manner of living," Herder anticipated what the discipline of anthropology would later come to do.[36] His thinking marked the work of a wide range of prominent nineteenth-century German intellectuals, scholars such as Wilhelm von Humboldt, Adolf Bastian, Wilhelm Dilthey, and Wilhelm Wundt, all decisive influences on the anthropology of Franz Boas, Bronisław Malinowski, and other canonical figures.[37] Take what Boas argued in a 1938 statement, "An Anthropologist's Credo," reflecting on the racial politics of the United States and Europe: "The study of human cultures should not lead to a relativistic attitude toward ethical standards. . . . The fundamental ethical point of view is that of the in-group, which must be expanded to include all humanity."[38]

The moral stakes of anthropology, for Boas, were in its promise to cultivate the sensibilities of those exposed to its manner of thinking, a way of approaching humanity less as object than as objective, a horizon of movement beyond the boundaries of a particular social environment and its history.[39] "If we desire to understand the development of human culture we must try to free ourselves of these shackles," Boas wrote. "This is possible only to those who are willing to adapt themselves to the strange ways of thinking and feeling of primitive people."[40]

Acts of terrible violence and injustice have been perpetrated in the name of humanity, and anthropologists too have been complicit in such deeds: think of the use of ethnography as a foundation for colonial rule in Asia and Africa, or the rise of a "dual use" anthropology in the twentieth-century United States that quietly served the interests of American Cold War military aggression.[41] All the same, it remains the case that such uses have not exhausted the meaning of humanity as an ideal, one that still is the bedrock of moral and political critique in the discipline. The history of this term reminds us that it need not be understood as opposed, by necessity, to the domain of the natural and nonhuman. This history also raises the question of how its legacies matter today, where and how their imprint remains. For the forms of imagination put into play by the idea of humanity as a moral horizon extend far beyond anthropology as a profession.

"Anthropos is that being who suffers from too many logoi," Paul Rabinow has observed, thinking through the many rival discourses that bend ideas of human possibility in profoundly different directions.[42] There is indeed scope for serious pathos or suffering in the tension between divergent imperatives and expectations. But everything turns, as Rabinow suggests, on how these discourses are put into practice, how they become elements of an ethos or way of life. This is not a matter of "applied" as opposed to basic anthropology but instead is a question about its pragmatic work in the world. "To attain perfect clearness in our thoughts of an object," William James argued in his lectures on pragmatism, "we need only consider what conceivable effects of a practical kind the object may involve—what sensations we are to expect from it, and what reactions we must prepare."[43] What if we were to try to imagine anthropology itself from the standpoint of such effects, and the range of their possible entailments?

Take this term, "humanity," and the question of whether it can be repurposed to meet the novel demands of this moment of ecological strife. Say we examine how others beyond the profession take up this essential feature of our thinking: concrete instances of anthropological reason already at work in the world and its human lives. Activists, artists, writers, for example: how do they conceive the horizons of a humanity to come? What forms of moral imagination and critique does anthropology inspire in other domains of practical life such as politics, art, and fiction? What ideas of anthropology effect "a difference which makes a difference" in these arenas, to borrow a phrase from Gregory Bateson, and can these practical effects, however modest, help us grasp what to do with that most vexed creature of ours, the human?[44]

We will have to wander farther afield now, beyond the professional bounds in which we have tarried thus far. And yet we remain ethnographers of anthropology at work, and the method too remains the same: seeking out mirrors in which to see ourselves anew.

THERE ARE PEOPLE from 192 countries milling about the cavernous exhibition hall of the Hawai'i Convention Center in Honolulu one Saturday evening in September. Voices carry far beyond the corrugated cardboard enclosures that divide the space into rival arenas, making for a deafening cacophony of earnest reportage. At the Water Pavilion, a lecture on mapping severe drought conditions in the western United States has just begun, while at the Business and Biodiversity Pavilion a young woman catalogues the achievements of an eco-tourism initiative in Taiwan. The Oceans and Islands Pavilion is gearing up for a presentation on marine plastic debris by the Canadian Wildlife Federation, while, nearby, wildlife biologists share the findings of a comprehensive census of African savannah elephant populations. A man in a feathered headdress looks on quietly as European bureaucrats speak of local "stakeholders" for forest management, while, at the U.S. Pavilion, American officials tout collaboration and chide those who would beat their own chests like silverback gorillas. At the adjacent Hawai'i Pacific Pavilion, meanwhile, an anthropologist recounts her work in revitalizing native dugout-canoe-building traditions in the Solomon Islands. There is a small but essential niche for anthropology at the 2016 World Conservation Congress (WCC) in Honolulu, for humankind's grasp of itself is at stake in these exchanges. As one anonymous participant declares in emphatic green marker on a graffiti wall planted into the center of the hall, "We are nature and nature is us!"

Taking place once every four years, the WCC is the signature event of the International Union for the Conservation of Nature (IUCN), founded in Switzerland in 1948. One of the most prominent and influential global environmental organizations, the IUCN has long been associated with government strategies of "coercive conservation," the endeavor to secure, often through highly militarized means, national parks and other protected areas

from any kind of habitation or resource use by local human populations.[45] Exclusionary approaches to nature conservation have met with much social criticism in recent years, and official statements from the IUCN now acknowledge that "understanding and addressing social equity in protected areas is important for ethical and moral reasons."[46]

Such concerns were especially prominent at the 2016 IUCN congress in Honolulu, "Planet at the Crossroads," where Hawai'i's own history as a Polynesian kingdom and former American colony was often invoked. The congress was inaugurated with a spectacular display of Hawai'ian ritual ceremony and dance, and sessions often began with chants and prayers in the Hawai'ian language. "*I am an endemic Hawai'ian species,*" a native Hawai'ian land manager noted in a talk one afternoon, twisting the sense of the nature at stake in these deliberations. "I was born here. I live here. This is where I thrive."

He had spoken in a session called "Indigenous Pacific Voices on the Nature/Culture Divide," one among hundreds in the "Forum" program of public presentations that made up the first half of the congress. As an anthropologist, I was struck by the very existence here of a panel on "the nature/culture divide" and the possibility of seeing it otherwise, given that the commonsensical quality of Western categories of nature and culture has been one of the most fundamental objects of critique in anthropological scholarship on the environment. "Western nature-culture constructs," Marilyn Strathern has argued, "revolve around the notion that the one domain is open to control or colonization by the other," an insight borne out by many studies of global conservation efforts and their difficulty in reconciling managerial imperatives with the customary practices of local people.[47] At the congress, sessions like this one were grouped into a number of "Journeys" through particular themes for participants to follow. I decided on the itinerary that included this session: the "Nature-Culture Journey."

"We are the vanguard of linking nature and culture," Andrew Potts of the International Council on Monuments and Sites told participants at the outset of this track, which he had organized, describing the endeavor as an "existential matter for the planet." I later learned that while he had read a fair amount of anthropology, the nature-culture problem for him was a task more institutional than metaphysical, concerning possible bridges between the different bureaucracies that governed "natural heritage" and "cultural heritage" sites. I thought of the "cosmopolitical" challenge that Isabelle Stengers has described, "a matter of imbuing political voices with the feeling that they do not master the situation they discuss, that the political arena is peopled with shadows of that which does not have a political voice."[48] What would it take for such shadows—the chief concern of anthropological engagements with conservation campaigns and institutions—to become visible here? What would it mean for such voices to be heard, for a more expansive and challenging sense of humanity to find a place in these debates?

It soon became clear that among the thousands of government officials, nongovernmental organization workers, activists, and scientists attending the congress, there were some who took the unity of nature and culture to pose a different kind of problem, one that was more imaginative and even ontological. At a session about protecting "sacred natural sites" from industrial activity, a Mongolian shaman spoke of an umbilical cord that bound humans together with the earth. Sitting beside him on the stage were indigenous leaders from several continents, including Patricia Gualinga, representing a Kichwa pueblo in the Ecuadorian rainforest. She described how moved she had been by the shaman's talk of spirits. "We are very similar," she said. "We believe that the beings who protect nature are connected by invisible threads in each part of the world, that we are not isolated, that we are connected from north to south." Gualinga had arrived at the panel with copies of a proposal to govern their territory as *kawsak sacha*, a "living forest," a message "aimed at the entire world with the goal of reaching the hearts and minds of human beings everywhere."[49] The organizations that orchestrated this particular session—the Sacred Land Film Project, the Gaia Foundation, Amazon Watch—worked closely with anthropologists, and, as it also happens, anthropologist Eduardo Kohn had translated the Kichwa proposal into English.

Such concrete proposals mattered at the congress, for the presentation sessions of the four-day forum would be followed by the Members' Assembly, in which the 1,300 government and nongovernment members of the IUCN would vote on over a hundred motions on topics, ranging from the protection of sharks and pangolins to renewable energy and environmental crimes. These decisions were not binding, but they made and matched precedents followed by other international environmental meetings; the WCC was the first such major global conference after the Paris climate summit of 2015, and it would be followed a few months later by the 2016 meeting of the Convention on Biological Diversity. There were "partial connections" between the arguments presented at the forum and the decisions made during the Members' Assembly, an officer of the United Nations Development Programme told me, invoking lessons from his own studies in anthropology with Marilyn Strathern. Active lobbying was afoot behind closed doors and along secluded hallways, and these ideas could travel in intangible ways.[50]

The indigenous activists sponsored by the Gaia Foundation spoke on behalf of Motion 26, which called on governments "to prohibit environmentally damaging industrial activities and infrastructure development" in all protected areas recognized by the IUCN, including "sacred natural sites and territories and areas conserved by indigenous peoples and local communities." A public communiqué written in the name of "indigenous guardians" from Hawai'i, Papua New Guinea, Ecuador, and elsewhere declared that cultural rites and ceremonial relationships with sacred places "have the capacity to change the physical nature of Mother Earth and to heal and enhance biodiversity." All the same, the tendency of governments around the world to capitulate to oil companies, mining interests, and other extractive industries lent a great deal of uncertainty to the fate of this motion. The United States, Australia, and Canada were hedging their support, and the CEO of the International Council on Mining and Metals was there to represent the largest companies in the industry. One of the most high-profile initiatives at the congress, meanwhile, was a collaboration with global financial institutions like Credit Suisse aimed at "creating new opportunities for return-seeking private investment in conservation."[51]

Advocates for indigenous rights at the WCC were placed in a difficult bind by such competing institutional priorities. "They paint this picture of us as not caring about trade, not being entrepreneurs," a Maori lawyer, Maru Samuels, told me. "For the contemporary conservation movement, poor indigenous peoples are the perfect environmentalists, they would only take what is necessary to feed their families that day." He attended on behalf of the Iwi Collective, a federation of Maori commercial fishing enterprises that had been fighting against a plan by the government of New Zealand to create a 600,000-square-kilometer marine sanctuary prohibiting commercial fishing. For Samuels, such measures recapitulated the nineteenth-century colonial erasure of Maori rights to land and sea, once again failing to recognize how deeply Maori aspirations were bound up with a healthy environment. At the WCC, Samuels was lobbying for amendments to the language of Motion 53, another high-profile measure that called for 30 percent of the world's oceans to be set aside as marine sanctuaries with "no extractive activities." The motion, he said, failed to acknowledge the *rangatiratanga*—the authority, or self-determination—of native peoples to make use of such places as they saw fit. "One of my missions will be to get that word into one of IUCN's documents," Samuels said with a rakish smile.

I was struck by the anthropological sensibility expressed in his interpretation of the congress: an acute sense of the limits of its dominant perspectives, the political and historical scaffolding of these limits, and the importance of transgressing them by mobilizing contrary experiences.[52] This was, in fact, one of the most essential ways in which anthropology seemed to be at work in the interstices of the congress, as a means of querying the adequacy of prevailing forms of conservation knowledge and practice, a vector for unusual connections and lateral displacements.[53] One afternoon, I attended a workshop, "Biocultural Creativity and Traditional Knowledge Documentation in the Pacific." The anthropologist James Leach of the University of Western Australia, together with Porer Nombo, a village leader from the Rai coast of northern Papua New Guinea, demonstrated a simple technique for making small notebooks to maintain handwritten records. People in the region were deeply concerned about the loss of traditional knowledge, Leach explained, but the social relationships that sustained its transmission were just as important as the fear of what might go unknown.[54] These handmade notebooks were designed to be passed on from person to person in local communities, affirming the significance of relational personhood, ensuring that "the knowledge could be kept in a form that generates relational connection." As Yat Paol, another indigenous delegate from the region, said, "We are going to save it our way, so that future generations know where to find it."

When we first met, and he learned that I was an anthropologist, Yat told me to read the work of Nikolai Miklouho-Maclay, a nineteenth-century Russian ethnographer who had lived on the Rai coast of New Guinea for years and had insisted that "representatives of these races have all the human rights" denied them by European imperialists.[55] Like most people at the Congress, Yat and his delegation from Papua New Guinea affirmed the importance of a common humanity. And yet their sense of this commonness took idiosyncratic turns. Melchior Ware, an elder from the same region, spoke one afternoon about the struggles of his village against a Chinese nickel mine. The former head of a government school, Melchior acknowledged the technological networks that had brought us here from distant places. All the same, he insisted, these differences of space and identity were nothing against the spiritual ties that bound us together as "articles" of a common soul. "We are connected with the waters, the air and space in which we live," he said earnestly to a small audience of listeners. "Please connect with us and be with us."

On the penultimate day of the congress, the Members' Assembly turned to voting on unresolved motions. Most of the motions had already been considered—and typically approved by overwhelming margins—through a preliminary voting process online, leaving only the most contentious proposals for further debate and discussion. The IUCN has a bicameral decision-making structure, with votes tabulated separately for both government and nongovernment members, and approval was needed from both sides. Motion 26 on extractive industries passed easily, with limited discussion and just a handful opposed on either side. The measure calling for an expansion of marine protected areas, Motion 53, also passed with strong majorities, though with vocal opposition from a few major countries like China and Japan. Its aim to protect 30 percent of the world's oceans from any extractive activity was now "subject to the rights of indigenous peoples and local communities," a hedge against global governance due in large part to vociferous negotiating by Maru Samuels of the Iwi Collective.

Samuels had wanted the motion to acknowledge that "no-take" strategies prohibiting any resource extraction were inconsistent with indigenous values and traditions, and he remained bitter about the final language of the motion. Still, the significance of these interventions was affirmed by several parties on the Assembly floor, including a representative of Kua, a native Hawai'ian environmental organization: "The new and progressive language of this motion to consider and engage in dialogue with indigenous people and local communities upfront is a proactive step in our collective relationships with nature and with each other. We believe that the power of *aloha* for one people, one ocean, and one *honua* is an important and unemphasized key to better stewardship of our only home and planet."

The Kua representative left these terms—*aloha* and *honua*—untranslated in her statement, letting listeners work out their implications for themselves. This small gesture embodies, for me, the spirit of anthropological intervention into the politics of the wcc. It was not simply a matter of harnessing local knowledge for better management, although this too was needed. Beyond such instrumental logic, there were many ways that anthropologists and their allies called attention to exceptions, remainders, equivocations, and human realities that demanded to be acknowledged without being fully understood. Their interventions were "cosmopolitical," in the sense proposed by Stengers: "The idea is precisely to slow down the construction of this common world, to create a space for hesitation."[56]

Everything at this global convention turned on the idea of one shared earth, and the need for a human collective that could recognize its importance. Yet, for at least some of us milling about in these hallways, there was also the sense that such a shared world could be forged more effectively in some other way, if people could open up their imagination of its nature and the nature of its inhabitants. For it did not suffice to fret over the limitations of human beings elsewhere, as much as this remains a bedrock impulse of environmentalism. These negotiations also put into play the possible humanity of those who pursued them, the need to sympathize with others who carried profoundly different ways of being into this vast arena. Here, in some modest way, anthropology had pragmatic value. There was political currency to its work with human possibility, a slender capacity to nurture otherwise impossible affinities.

SAUSALITO, 2004. A peculiar kind of exhibition—something between art, science, fantasy, and activist intervention—is unveiled one November day at the San Francisco Bay Model Visitor Center. Fixed to the wall are long rows of bottle caps and combs, cigarette lighters and shotgun wads, all made of plastic and strangely pitted and weathered. Nearby is a series of narrow tubes crammed with brightly colored plastic fragments, carefully sealed and mounted vertically with the semblance of geological core samples. These are the remnants of a bygone civilization, the wall text tells us, placing visitors in the distant future year of 2855 CE. Researchers from the future, it seems, have found and excavated a unique and anomalous stratigraphic layer in the earth's crust, what they call a "Plasticene Discontinuity." The findings invite speculation about the people of this "Age of Grease," whose fixation on hydrocarbons and rivers of indestructible plastic waste drove them ultimately to ruin:

> There is much evidence that they were a warlike people whose children actually played with tiny armed men acting out battles from the continuous warfare of the Plasticene. The curious array of rectangular boxes were fuel containers used to ignite a very popular drug which was drawn into the lungs to enter the bloodstream. There is evidence the use of this drug was a signal that the user was very brave as the drug was at once highly addictive and caused several debilitating diseases. From this we imagine these were a very tough-minded people.[57]

The installation, put up by the Bay Area–based artist couple Richard Lang and Judith Selby Lang, anticipated by well over a decade arguments now made by earth scientists, that the swelling plastic debris of our time—the billions of tons of bottles, brushes, wrappers, and countless other things buried in landfills, littered on coastlines, and settling onto seabeds—is an essential "stratigraphic indicator of the Anthropocene."[58] Lang and Lang share their archaeological sensibility with many other contemporary artists who work with plastic detritus, taking these abandoned everyday objects as ciphers for the societies that cast them away so lightly.[59]

Works like *The Plasticene Discontinuity* also playfully evoke broader currents of affinity between anthropology and contemporary art. "Artists increasingly engage in fieldwork practices," Arnd Schneider and Christopher Wright note.[60] Practices of field-based inquiry and documentation appeal to many artists for the same reason that sensory modes of expression appeal to anthropologists: as ways of working more concretely to unsettle familiar ideas of humanity and its limits. As Hal Foster observed in an influential 1995 critique of ethnographic aspirations in contemporary art, "anthropology is prized as the science of *alterity*."[61]

When I first set out to meet Richard and Judith in early 2016, their house in Forest Knolls, California, was unmistakable: it was the one with the giant yellow plastic buoy resting against a tree, overflowing with pale blue ovoid fishing floats like a hoard of eggs from a petrochemical robin. Comic reinventions of plastic trash were everywhere inside, clearly a matter of both art and life. The installation at the Bay Model Visitor Center went up shortly after the couple married at the Burning Man festival in Nevada; Judith wore a dress of white plastic shards and a shawl stitched together from dry-cleaning bags. The pair shared a fascination with things that washed up unpredictably on the seashore, and their most notable collaborative works are arrangements of such detritus, photographed and magnified many times over against a stark white backdrop. *Spiff*, for example, a print that was traveling with an international art show on ocean plastic when I saw it that year at a gallery in San Jose, California, gathers up a plastic bottle, spoon, and toothbrush, along with a piece of Astroturf, part of a toy-truck wheel, and other assorted debris.[62] Beautifully enlarged to fill out a frame three feet across, the image (reproduced on the cover of this book) captures minuscule nicks and hollows in the surfaces of these objects and a gentle mottling of their synthetic hues, a patina attesting to their lengthy life at sea.

For almost two decades, Richard and Judith have trekked up and down a thousand-yard stretch of Northern California coastline called Kehoe Beach, picking out all of the objects they work with from the sands of this single place alone. Part of the Point Reyes National Seashore and accessible only from one isolated road, Kehoe Beach presents a beautiful landscape of verdant dunes and crashing surf. Still, due to its position just north of the San Francisco Bay and wider patterns of North Pacific currents, plastic litter lands here daily from throughout the Bay Area and even from Asian cities thousands of miles away.

I had the chance to visit Kehoe Beach with the artist couple one August morning in 2016. "Plastic is the excrement of oil," Richard intoned, quoting Norman Mailer with mock gravity as we walked along a trail down to the shore. He and Judith showed me how easily one could overlook the countless manmade objects buried underfoot. Working our way up and down the beach over the next couple of hours, collecting sacks in hand, we found bottle caps, knotted bags, clothing tags, and bits of polypropylene rope and netting, but also countless tiny and anonymous fragments nestled among the seaweed and pebbles. Judith pointed out many "nurdles," industrial raw materials in the shape of tiny plastic pellets, which they had first noticed some years back when staking out four-foot-square plots to excavate the shoreline as carefully as possible.

All told that morning, after just a few hours of gathering, we managed to find an astonishing 774 pieces of plastic debris working their way into the depths of the sand. The sedimentary layers of the sandstone cliffs overlooking Kehoe Beach had inspired *The Plasticene Discontinuity* and its geological imagination. And indeed, what the artists have found washed up here over the years are tangible remnants of our time and its aspirations: to-go cups from a restless population forever on the move, the lid of a ballot box from a hard-fought San Francisco election, even pieces of a sunken America's Cup yacht prototype, built from an experimental carbon polymer for the Silicon Valley entrepreneur Larry Ellison. The artists gathered these materials like anthropologists of contemporary life; such artifacts would anchor the cultural portraits they made.

Over their years of collecting, Richard and Judith estimate, Kehoe Beach has given them more than three tons of such plastic things. The material goes to a barn below their house, where it is washed and sorted by color and kind. I spent a few hours there one afternoon, examining their collection, most of it stacked in cardboard boxes with labels like "Blue," "Pink," "Shoes," and "Cutlery." At first it was overwhelming, sifting through the sheer mass and variation of what they had found: the toy astronauts, guns, and robots; the heap of grimy toothbrushes and the lids imprinted with Chinese characters; the piles of broken containers like tinkling plastic potshards; the lawn sprayer valve and the tag from a long-gone shipment of food. Then I began to sense the consistencies in what was here: the distinctive smell released by a box of tattered balloons, for example, or the way that each piece in a box of burnt and molten plastic rubbish had congealed into a unique approximation of organic form. I thought of what Judith had said of the "pull tabs" that are ripped out of fresh cartons of milk: put them together, side by side, and "a whole world of 'pulltabness' reveals itself. Each piece of plastic contains that revelation."

It was this possibility that *The Plasticene Discontinuity* sought to kindle, the idea of being drawn in unexpectedly by commonplace things. The exhibition recast their ongoing excavations at Kehoe Beach as work by archaeologists from the distant future. Carefully laying out sets of lighters, toothbrushes, plastic balls, and other banal items, side by side among many other objects of their own kind, the work encouraged a lighthearted examination of "the creative impulse of Plasticene peoples." There were echoes here of

(Fig.A) **THE PLASTICENE DISCONTINUITY** 2855, CE

Courtesy of Richard Lang and Judith Selby Lang.

Horace Miner's classic satire of the "Nacirema," in the exploration of "a fastidious and vain people" obsessed with products for personal hygiene.[63] But the anthropological vantage point gave the artists a unique way of engaging such habits in a mood both bemused and generous at the same time. "Look closely and you can see the mark of all the little balls," the exhibition advised viewers, describing the "little translucent florets" that would have carried explosive metal pellets for the bygone humans who "lived by hunting animals and eating them." Presented in this manner, the heedlessly disposable plastic shotgun shells of our time—cast by the millions into forests and wetlands with the firing of these guns, with well over a thousand found by the artists on Kehoe Beach alone—became things to approach with a measure of sympathy and not just horror.

"Works of art are the only media of complete and unhindered communication between man and man that can occur in a world full of gulfs and walls that limit community of experience," John Dewey wrote in a 1934 book, *Art as Experience*, that Richard and Judith keep handy at their home in Forest Knolls.[64] Dewey's interest in art as a means of sensory interchange with others resonates with the aesthetic effects that the artists pursued in their work. They are often asked, "Why do you make it so beautiful?" Judith recounted. "Beauty attracts people. There is pleasure, and then, 'Oh my god, all this is plastic!' The experience of beauty makes a person more receptive, it cracks people open." As self-described children of the 1960s, she and Richard admitted that they sometimes lapsed into anger and bitterness. The plastic artifacts they work with have harrowing lives at sea; they once crafted a quirky sea monster from hundreds of pounds of fishing net, found in the belly of a beached sperm whale that must have suffered an excruciating death. The humor in such works, however, offered a different way of conveying the gravity of such problems. "You can't be hateful and expect things to change," Judith explained. "Hate brings about intransigence."

At the Oakland Museum of California, Judith and Richard have a longstanding exhibition aimed at schoolchildren, called *An Ocean of Plastic*. The exhibit encourages reflection on consumer habits and their consequences by using the things that are found on the beach. "Is it possible to be plastic free?" a board asks on a back wall. "NOT w/ Donald Trump!" one student had declared on a Post-it note when I visited the museum in early 2016. I spent some time paging through a notebook of stories written by young visitors, about plastic mystery objects of their own imagination. Some were rather didactic, while others ridiculed the exercise as children will do. I was struck, though, by how many of them entered into the scene of the beach and the myriad lives brought together on its sands. Take this story, for example, of a plastic water bottle from China once used, it seems, by "a teenage gangster in San Diego":

> The kid was walking down the street right by the ocean with her friends. She drops it on the ground since there are no trash cans in the area. A few days later their is a wind storm and the bottle is swept into the ocean. Over the next several months the bottle is tossed around the ocean swept through storms until . . . a hungry whale sees it reflecting off the sun and eats it! Eventually, a few years later when the whale died, it washed up on Kehoe Beach. A few marine Biologists generously gave it to a high school class to dissect. When the kid began to disect the stomach he found the bottle!

Consider how this story takes us through the experience of a young woman, then a plastic bottle, then a whale, then some humans once again. It is this kind of imaginative movement that strikes me as most consequential, in anthropological terms, about the kind of work that artists like Richard Lang and Judith Selby Lang do: the possibility of reaching with sympathy into the lives of different others, and thereby opening the prospect of living profoundly otherwise.

"A thousand years from now," Judith speculated, "we will look back at these people, at ourselves and say, 'Did we really need these little plastic cheese spreaders? What are the things that make us human and really enhance our lives?'" She and her partner asked such questions as artists and activists, not as anthropologists per se. And yet the anthropological impulse propelling their efforts had everything to do with their imagination of this humanity to come. Their work, like our own, was founded on the vision of an exit, some other way of living beyond the most proximate and pervasive habits of the world at hand.

SOMETIME EARLY IN the year 1980, the novelist Ursula K. Le Guin receives a fan letter. And yet the letter isn't actually addressed to Le Guin, but instead to "Faxe," a minor character in one of her most beloved books, *The Left Hand of Darkness*, first published in 1969. Inked with fine calligraphy onto several cream-colored sheets, the missive runs as follows:

Dear Faxe,

When I first read <u>The Left Hand of Darkness</u> some eight or nine years ago, I thought I heard the voice of your father, Alfred Kroeber, coaching you from the wings as you constructed the myths and stories, the crafts and ceremonies of Karhide into the nearly harmonious whole that marks a viable true culture (Orgoreyn never seemed so concrete, although I feel I know the Orgota better than the inhabitants of Seattle; but perhaps I expect too much of the people of Seattle—they should be as exciting, as stimulating, as awe-inspiring as the site they inhabit).

You made Karhide more real to me than, say, Hungary, a place I suppose to exist, though I have never been there; I feel as though I could find my way around the old capital of Rer more easily than around the old capital of Buda, no matter how confusing Genly found it.

The crossing of the Kargav still affects me much as my first crossing of the Cascades at Naches Pass, when Tahoma, that magic mountain, awed me into speechlessness when it suddenly loomed high above me.

I did not recognize the voice of your father speaking through Estraven, however, because you had camouflaged his appearance very well. It was only when I began to listen to Estraven as I was writing this letter that I recognized his ways of speaking.

Your father was a master of shifgrethor. I heard him blithely conceding to some Marxist students at Columbia the possibility that his hard-fought-out concepts of culture, culture area and what I am now calling the natural lifetimes of cultures (because I have forgotten what he called it) might well be in error; but in the process he exposed the puerility and the dogmatism of the Marxist preconceptions. I heard the same voice speaking to the Orgota Commensals at their banquets.

Perhaps you may be curious why I waited so long to write you. Well, it was because you seemed to have the numen of a Weaver wrapped around you, and I feared to disturb you for anything so trivial as a fan letter.

But yesterday I read The Language of the Night for the first time (I shall read, pore over, dissect, reassemble, fight and agree with parts of it many times more), and it reminded me that Faxe touches divinity only temporarily and is human most of the time.

The letter goes on like this, passing through many more of Le Guin's works and then closing with the words "Gratefully yours, Klod the Barbarian."[65] This signature, and the heading that inaugurates the letter—"To Elfland from Poughkeepsie"—both play on an essay in Le Guin's *Language of the Night*, in which the author describes fantasy as "surrealistic, super-realistic, a heightening of reality."[66] And indeed, this is precisely the way in which the Barbarian's letter takes stock of one of the most famous filial ties between fiction and anthropology. Ursula K. Le Guin becomes Faxe the Weaver, a figure "as limpid and unfathomable as a well of very clear water," whose powers of prophecy convey an insight essential to storytelling and anthropology alike, that "the only thing that makes life possible is permanent, intolerable uncertainty: not knowing what comes next."[67] Alfred L. Kroeber, the distinguished anthropologist who was her father, assumes the visage of a nobleman of Le Guin's fictional planet of Gethen, an adept at its games of political prestige, or *shifgrethor*. Gethen's nation of Karhide and its an-

To Elfland from Poughkeepsie

Dear Faxe,
　　　　　When I first read
The Left Hand of Darkness some
eight or nine years ago, I thought
I heard the voice of your father,
Alfred Kroeber, coaching you from
the wings as you constructed the
myths and stories, the crafts and
ceremonies of Karhide into the
nearly harmonious whole that
marks a viable true culture (Orgoreyn never seemed so concrete, although

cient capital Rer, the Orgota nation of Orgoreyn and the Commensals who run its government, the imposing Kargav mountain range and the journey the interplanetary envoy Genly Ai takes across it: all these things somehow seem more real, more concrete, more familiar even than the places shared by writers and readers on a planet known as Earth.

The letters to Le Guin held in the University of Oregon archives, where I stumbled across this one, reveal readers entranced by her prolific body of novels, poems, and essays. Striving for words writerly and engaging in their own right, correspondents sent her poetry, fiction of their own, drawings, missives in code and made-up languages, sometimes just exuberant prose. The letters convey the vividness of the places conjured up by Le Guin's science fiction; as one fan wrote in 1972, "Please keep dreaming alternative worlds. They make the one we are stuck in so much richer."[68] It is also striking how many of these readers discerned the anthropological spirit at work in her novels. As one young woman wrote from Switzerland, explaining why Le Guin had led her to study anthropology in Neuchâtel, "With your books I have found out that science fiction *is* anthropology. To describe another world, it is learning about our own world."[69] What could it mean, to insist upon this likeness?

I first encountered Le Guin's novels as an undergraduate at Amherst College. I went on to study anthropology at the University of California, Berkeley, department founded by her father in 1901, passing in and out of Kroeber Hall each day. Kroeber's closest Papago and Yurok collaborators would stay with his family at the Napa Valley ranch where they spent each summer in the 1930s and 1940s, and these daily experiences with her "Indian uncles," Le Guin later recalled, gave her "the sense that nothing and no one is irredeemably foreign—alien—Other."[70] In a lecture that she gave in the Berkeley anthropology department on the occasion of its one hundredth anniversary— a talk that I missed, as I was in South India for dissertation fieldwork at the time—the novelist acknowledged that "my memories of these two Native American friends are hedged with caution and thorned with fear," for she knew almost nothing about their personal history and political condition. And yet, she reflected, matters as small as the discovery that birthdays meant nothing to these men, that time itself was different for them, may have been "the soil from which the cultural relativism of my fictions would grow and flourish."[71]

Le Guin's mother, Theodora Kroeber, immersed herself in the tragic story of another California native, Ishi, the subject of her bestselling book.[72] Not surprisingly, with such heritage behind them, Le Guin's books teem with anthropologists. Take, for example, her stories set in the "Hainish" universe of multiple human populations on far-flung planets, works that typically trail outsiders with anthropological curiosity about the people they have landed among. The first of her novels, *Rocannon's World*, tells the story of an interplanetary ethnographer, opening with his survey of "hominoid" species on the world of Fomalhaut II. A later book, *The Dispossessed*, follows a physicist's journey to a foreign planet where he often reflects on "what [it] might be like to be on one's own in a society where men did not trust one another, where the basic moral assumption was not mutual aid, but mutual aggression."[73] As with ethnographers on Earth—or Terra, as our world is known there— these lonely figures serve at times as emissaries of a larger political order with murky ambitions, such as Captain Raj Lyubov in *The Word for World Is Forest*, tasked with studying the diminutive natives of a verdant planet colonized for its timber resources. Some take on the work of salvage, characters like Sutty in *The Telling*, who wrestles with the pace of change on a postcontact world, "to learn what I can about some of the old ways . . . the arts and beliefs and customs that flourished on Aka before my people came here."[74]

Alfred L. Kroeber's anthropological engagement with "wrecks of cultures" on the frontiers of the American West, Le Guin has acknowledged, was both "an act of imperialism" and "an act of human solidarity."[75] As a "granddaughter of the American frontier," the novelist has described her own task as an effort "to listen to the voices from the other side."[76] Think of what happens to the narrator of *The Left Hand of Darkness*, Genly Ai, charged with bringing the people of Gethen into an interplanetary alliance with remote, unseen worlds by appealing to "their strong though undeveloped sense of humanity, of human unity."[77] For the Gethenians, whose uniquely cyclical makeup takes them gradually and continuously back and forth between male and female physiology, the alien Genly is at first "an oddity, a sexual freak," dismissed as not even human because he remains so stubbornly male.[78] But then after years of his sojourn among the Gethenians, it is his own shipmates from other worlds, with genders akin to ours, that now seem inhuman to him: "They all looked strange to me, men and women, well as I knew them. Their voices sounded strange: too deep, too shrill. They were like a troupe of great, strange animals, of two different species; great apes with intelligent eyes, all of them in rut."[79]

"Every understanding of another culture is an experiment with our own," Roy Wagner wrote in *The Invention of Culture*, an insight essential to the "ontological turn" in contemporary anthropology.[80] The endeavor indeed involves working with "fictions," as Eduardo Viveiros de Castro has put it in *Cannibal Metaphysics*: not untruths as such, but the contrary realities that come into focus when starkly foreign ideas are taken to make sense, and their consequences followed through in earnest. "It is not the task of explaining the world of the other," Viveiros de Castro writes, "but that of multiplying our world."[81] We can see this happening quite profoundly with the novels written by authors like Ursula K. Le Guin, in the imaginative possibilities they pull together and propel.[82] And when we attend in particular to their anthropological inflections, to the fate of the human in these stories, we may glimpse a moral project of empathy at work, one related in spirit to anthropology itself. "Science fiction," as Le Guin once said, "allows me to help people get out of their cultural skins and into the skins of other beings."[83]

The significance of such movement was conveyed in a poignant manner by a symposium on Le Guin at the University of Oregon in late 2016. Younger women writers of science fiction spoke about how they came to see for the first time, with her novels, that women actually existed in the future. A transgender man recalled one of the most vertiginous sentences in *The Left Hand of Darkness*—"The king was pregnant"—in chronicling his own experience as a pregnant man in transition, his shivering through labor in Minneapolis rooms as icy as the halls of Karhide. "Can we make justice the most pleasurable experience that humans can have?" an African American writer and activist from Detroit asked, evoking the anarchist utopia of Le Guin's planet Anarres to make sense of her own city's experiments with alternative ways of being.

Le Guin was present for half of the symposium, listening quietly and writing busily to herself on a small pad of paper. I introduced myself during one break as an adoring fan. I told her that I'd just taught *Changing Planes* as a work of speculative anthropology, and that I'd studied anthropology in Kroeber Hall. "So you've been under the weight of my family for a long time," she replied with a laugh. Already somewhat frail and infirm (Le Guin passed on a little over a year later), she did not address the audience in that hall. And yet you could see that the alien characters and places she had conjured were already part of this one here, tangible presences that had transformed what all of us thought about the human and its limits. "Beings of fiction populate the world," Bruno Latour reminds us.[84]

Once the symposium ended, I sat down for a long conversation with another one of the speakers, Grace Dillon, who teaches in the Indigenous Nations Studies program at Portland State University. Anishinaabe by heritage, she had grown up on an anarchist commune in the Midwest, where a visiting bookmobile sometimes dropped off books by Le Guin. Grace had spoken earlier that day of a kind of "human Milky Way" that gathers together persons of all kinds like beads on a chain: human ancestors and descendants, but also "animal persons, plant persons, and, with science fiction, machine persons." She found herself drawn to the kindred and expansive sense of personhood expressed in Le Guin's novels. And this resonance helped with her own efforts to sketch the contours of "indigenous futurism," a genre defined by Dillon's pathbreaking anthology of Native American science fiction, *Walking the Clouds*.[85] "If you are thinking of something, you are also willing it into being, it actually comes about," Grace told me, describing the Anishinaabe idea of *inaendumowiin*, creative imagination. Listening to her tales, I began to see more fully how fiction mattered in the world, how the passage of these stories from person to person to person could actually foment new ways of life.

City of Illusions, one of Le Guin's first novels, begins as a man with yellow, catlike eyes finds himself in the midst of an unknown settlement of forest dwellers. You might wonder with some suspicion why this unnamed world has pine and hemlock trees, herds of sheep and cattle, expanses of a landscape the novelist calls prairie. And then you read, midway through, that there are also ancient remnants here of a time that passed some three thousand years before, that "fragments of pottery, flecks of colored glass and plastic were thick in the spongy ground around these places."[86] You begin to realize that you are still on Earth, "a great lovely garden gone all to weeds and wilderness," long past "the Age of Cities" and "the Age of War."[87] And so you continue to wander across the face of the world with this cat-eyed foreigner, meeting herdsmen who land their raw-beef repasts with hand-lasers, island natives "entirely absorbed in sailing, swimming and sex," and a telepathic race masquerading as demons to lord over them all.[88]

What is it to gaze at them through the peculiar yellow orbs of this stranger? Their humanity is vexing, yes, these peoples of an Earth yet to come, but make no mistake, what is truly at stake here are the horizons of our own perception now.

IN 2005, ROY SCRANTON, a private in the U.S. Army, returns to Fort Sill, Oklahoma, from a tour of duty in Baghdad. "I thought I had made it out," he later recalls. But he can't shake the sense of a crisis more endemic and pervasive, the desperate overdrive of the civilization that had dispatched him across the world to battle for petroleum and a phantom security. "The grim future I'd seen in Baghdad had come home: not terrorism, not WMDS, but the machinery of civilization breaking down, unable to recuperate from shocks to its system," Scranton writes in his searing polemic, *Learning to Die in the Anthropocene*. "To survive as a soldier, I had to learn to accept the inevitability of my own death. For humanity to survive in the Anthropocene, we need to learn to live with and through the end of our current civilization."[89] Pursuit of such lessons would lead the veteran to study the literature of war and heroism at Princeton University, and eventually to take up the vocation of a writer. "In order to adapt to this strange new world," Scranton says, "we need a new vision of who 'we' are. We need a new humanism."[90]

This essay has explored anthropology as an impetus to such imagination. We have seen how activists, artists, and writers can work with the anthropological inclination to think and dream the human in contrary terms, even in the face of catastrophic dispossession and neglect. We have also seen how the expressive forms proper to these domains of practice—public speech, art, and fiction—do more than simply depict what is or ought to be elsewhere. Instead, they help to bring these possibilities into being, into reality, through the germinal and generative powers invested in their communicative forms. A cultural artifice can indeed be understood, as Michael Fischer writes in *Anthropological Futures*, like an "experimental system" that "allows new realities to be seen and engaged as its own parameters are changed."[91] Where does this leave our own signal mode of expression in anthropology, that practice of experience and experiment we call ethnography? If anthropology concerns the possible genesis of a humanity yet to come, as I have argued here, what of the *ethnos* or "people" that ethnography seeks to conjure? What does an ethnography intend for the world and its troubles, in moral and political terms?

I had the chance to think through these questions concretely a couple of years ago, in teaching an undergraduate course about ethnography at Johns Hopkins. The students kept field diaries and followed, over many weeks, topics such as the art of brewing at a local Baltimore coffeehouse and fitness culture at the campus gym. When it came time for them to write up their observations, however, my co-teacher, Bürge Abiral, and I found ourselves perplexed.[92] The students needed instructions. But what exactly did we want them to write in the name of *ethnography*? After the many modes and styles we had examined over the semester, how could we possibly settle on one definition of this term? We masked our dilemma with a bit of chicanery, asking each student to write an ethnographic account and then make sense of it by articulating their own understanding of ethnography. When the papers came in, we were struck by their consistency: so many of them put forward the idea of a transformative encounter, what can happen to oneself when drawn into another world as ethnographer, or as reader. "Ethnography acts as a portal," one student wrote. "An ethnography is a personal account that a reader is able to step into and make his or her own. Honoring the human nature and natural bias of the ethnographer makes the experience all the more real; the reader participates in a raw human experience."

The sense for ethnography that the students had developed was anchored in six recent texts we read together over the course of the semester. Looking back once again at those books now, I see why such an understanding of ethnography would have made sense to them. For all these books, written in diverse ways about unrelated topics, sought to put readers in the company of foreign beings with whom they would find something unexpected in common.

— "If you could make the soil liquid and transparent and walk into the ground," Anna Tsing muses in *The Mushroom at the End of the World*, inviting readers to imagine a hidden realm of social life not altogether unlike our own, "you would find yourself surrounded by nets of fungal hyphae. Follow fungi into that underground city, and you will find the strange and varied pleasures of interspecies life."[93]

— "Follow the contents of your garbage bag, recycling bin, or toilet and they will lead you to people and places to whom you are unknowingly connected," Joshua Reno writes in *Waste Away*, taking readers into the day-to-day operations of a Michigan landfill and the daily lives of its workers. "The movement of waste elsewhere creates a distancing effect—a separation between waste workers and waste makers—yet what goes on at landfills continues to shape our lives, behind our backs and beneath our notice."[94]

— In *Rendering Life Molecular*, Natasha Myers considers the idea that beneath our notice, matter itself may be fundamentally alive, like us. We enter into this possibility with crystallographers like Diane, and their calisthenic struggles to understand the molecules they work with: "With one arm bent over her head, another wrapping around the front of her body, her neck crooked to one side, and her body twisting, she expressed the strain that would be felt by the misshapen protein if it had to take this form."[95]

— A recent book of mine, *Reel World*, suggests approaching the world "as a flux of images, and every film as an experiment with its reality." The book asks readers to imagine a world shared with the characters of a film or with the filmmakers who give them flesh and form: "Say we plunged into the depths of some of their experiments—what would happen to us, and to our understanding of this life in a world of images?"[96]

— "The annihilation of bodies in the desert is never meant to be seen," Jason De León writes in *The Land of Open Graves*. The book gives the wrenching image of a migrant's body he encountered sprawled on a hill near the U.S.-Mexico border, and then the story of the woman she once was and the family that once was hers. "The whole world has dreams, but sometimes those same dreams can destroy a life," Maricela's brother-in-law Christian reflects. "We leave home with hope, but we never know when we are going to encounter death there in the desert. It is such an ugly way to die, all alone."[97]

— Lisa Stevenson relates the dream of a young friend in *Life Beside Itself*. "As she told the dreams her voice had its own force. It lifted away from her body. She was *telling* me something—the filaments of a story reached outward," she writes. Then the author's voice also slips into a mood of reverie, enveloping readers in the ambiguity of Inuit life and death, dissolving the boundary between their experience and ours. "I wonder, then, if we don't lend enough importance to the grammar of a life. Do we at least begin to create a world for ourselves through simply stating that something, anything, *is*?"[98]

Each of these books, in its own way, acknowledges the violence and neglect lodged within the very category of human being, in the many distinctions that the category implies between those worthy and unworthy of attention. The anonymous care of a suicide prevention line, for example, founded, as Stevenson argues, on the abstract idea of a common humanity stripped of particular markers or qualifiers, can make it far more difficult to understand an individual's suffering: "No individual bonds are established, no specific links between people strengthened."[99]

But let us heed as well that other horizon of humanity still at stake in *Life Beside Itself*, as with all of these other books, anchored in the possibility of a concrete and emergent collectivity: not humanity as a species, but humanity as a moral feeling of responsiveness, as the sense of a fate shared with others unlike oneself. For all these books, like the enterprise of ethnography more generally, grasp for an elusive whole and seek to draw their readers into that fullness. *This is a world, yes, this other one here, but what if this were the world? How would that change your sense of what you are, the universe and community to which you belong?* Such works are engaged, in other words, in a pragmatic rather than strictly representational register, seeking to put the human particularity of those who encounter them into question, and therefore in motion.

If this is indeed what ethnography does, then the *ethnos* or the "people" of ethnography must be fundamentally open. Public appropriation of anthropological findings is often seen to involve a reification of cultural difference, an essentialization of who "we" are, as opposed to others elsewhere. This may happen, but this isn't all that an ethnography can accomplish. The transgressive power of ethnography lies in its ability to fashion a novel domain of collective experience, one that may span the distance between anthropologist, subject, and public alike. Ethnography can summon a "people to come," to borrow a phrase from Gilles Deleuze and Félix Guattari: "not the one that claims to be pure but rather an oppressed, bastard, lower, anarchical, nomadic, and irremediably minor race," provoking the creation, in other words, of an otherwise unlikely people, the emergence of an otherwise difficult alliance.[100] This is the political promise of the experience that ethnography carries from place to place, of the stories that pass through its portals between one world and yet another.

An author, Deleuze suggested, may be understood as "a true collective agent, a collective leaven, a catalyst," one who works with "the seeds of the people to come."[101] With this idea of an author as agent, leaven, and catalyst, or indeed as cultivator working with seeds, we return to an older yet enduring sense of culture, culture not as object, but as process.[102] *Kultur* can be likened to "the cultivation of the soil," Herder noted in the late eighteenth century, making sense of a term that derived originally from the Latin verb *colere*, to till, tend, and care for.[103] This work of cultivation extends to the vocation of the writer and thinker; as Herder reflected in an early essay on popular philosophy, "I am planting thoughts and prospects. I leave it to others to raise these seeds, and to make them trees, and perhaps also to gather fruit."[104] At stake in such efforts was the vision of a people that did not yet exist, the vexed sense of a community to come. "I shall lead my readers onto a knoll," Herder proposed, "and show them how in the valley and on the plain creatures stray about that are so diverse that they hardly have a common name left; however, they are our fellow brothers, and their history is the history of our nature."[105]

What kinds of creatures are these, that the ethnographer asks us to look on as brothers from an imaginary knoll? What would it take to approach their nature as an original contribution to a history we might share with them? The shadow of Western racism and imperialism looms over this problem, for, as Aimé Césaire observed, "the colonizer . . . gets into the habit of seeing the other man as *an animal*, accustoms himself to treating him like an animal, and tends objectively to transform *himself* into an animal." Yet, for all this, the Martinican poet did not reject humanism, calling instead for "a true humanism—a humanism made to the measure of the world."[106] Nor did he repudiate ethnography altogether, which might seek to place and register each side by side with the others of the world—"I defy the craniometer," Césaire declared—but could also sustain the idea of a more radical and unsettling kinship with other kinds.[107]

> To leave:
> As there are hyena-men and panther-men, I would be a jew-man,
> a kaffir-man,
> a Hindu-man-from-Calcutta
> a Harlem-man-who-does-not-vote
>
> a famine artist, an insult-man, a torture man, you can at any moment lay hold of him, pummel him with blows, kill him—actually kill him—without having to account to anyone, without having to make excuses to anyone
> a jew-man
> a pogrom-man
> a puppy-dog
> a beggar-bum
>
> but does one ever kill Chagrin, as fair as the startled face of an English lady who peers into her soup tureen to find a Hottentot skull?

I would rediscover the secret code of grand communications and of grand conflagrations. I would say hurricane. I would say river. I would say tornado. I would say leaf. I would say tree. I would be soaked with all the rains, moistened with all the dews. I would circulate like frenetic blood on the slow current in the eye of storming words, becoming mad horses, or fresh progeny, or blood clots, or traces of a temple or precious stones far enough in the earth to discourage miners. He who failed to grasp my words would no more readily grasp the roaring of a tiger.[108]

Imagine an ethnography open to the spell of these words. Imagine one that would not flinch to dissolve into this cosmic flux. Imagine one that could approach all such beings as kin. Imagine one that could culture the capacity for such humanity, that would seek to cultivate such humanity, that would work with the moral vision and imagination of people as it found them, whether as readers, listeners, interlocutors, or fellow citizens.

All the most reckless and imperious things ever done in the name of anthropology begin here, yes. And yet this remains a beginning, the seed of an anthropology to come.

Coda
The Anthropologist as Critic

Anthropology promises the joy of unexpected communion. Anthropology also holds out the prospect of a lingering unease, a persistent sense of something unwell in the world. For with every feeling of fullness in the company of others comes that darker gift of anthropological perspective, that nagging question—*The sense of completeness in this life, for whom?*

It was such a feeling of "malaise" that led Gerald Berreman to challenge the smug complacency of American professional anthropology in the late 1960s and early 1970s. Blithely relying on government sponsorship to gather field data from contested arenas of global Cold War politics, many social scientists had been made into unwitting agents of American militarism. In 1968, Berreman resigned from a large-scale Himalayan border research project supported increasingly by the Pentagon. He and other members of the

American Anthropological Association's Committee on Ethics challenged the clandestine arrangements that put certain anthropologists in the service of American counterinsurgency campaigns in Southeast Asia.[1] "We . . . ask," Berreman wrote in an important contribution to the 1972 volume *Reinventing Anthropology*, "if we do not have a positive responsibility, not simply to the truth, but to the courageous exposition of the truth and to acting upon the implications of that truth."[2] Far from a distant and neutral reflection on the world, anthropological knowledge was itself a force *in* the world, for better or worse, an element in its struggles.

Like so many other students of anthropology, I too was drawn into the discipline with the politics of social change in mind. I applied to graduate school in the mid-1990s from a village-based rural development organization in South India, relying on the rickety old manual typewriter we used in the office to send out grant applications and progress reports. I enrolled in an environmental studies program at the University of California, Berkeley, hoping for further training in the sustainable development work I'd begun to pursue as a volunteer in India. But then as my questions took me further and further into the conundrums of human motivation and the real circumstances of its transformation, I found myself drifting toward anthropology, and I eventually transferred into the department.

Berreman was still around, on the verge of retirement, trailed by legends of his political work during the Vietnam War era. Laura Nader gave us diagnoses in class of the difficulty that Americans had with overt conflict and argument. Nancy Scheper-Hughes had recently published her impassioned manifesto for a "barefoot" and militant anthropology among the poor. Paul Rabinow, whose office in Kroeber was just down the hall from hers, had responded with a vision for collaborative work among equals that "usually requires wearing shoes."[3] The department was highly charged and famously fraught. Every professor seemed an avatar of some strain of politics, a larger-than-life embodiment of some particular way of conceiving and engaging the strife of the times. I wound up studying under the supervision of Donald Moore, whose attention to cultural politics and postcolonial criticism offered a way to make sense of the ideas of nature and environment that I had encountered on the ground in rural India.

There are indeed many ways of being a critic in anthropology. And we would do well to examine the "affective commitments" that propel these critical endeavors, as argued by Saba Mahmood, who had also come to Berkeley in those years.[4] There is the idea of the academy as a singular space for free and impartial inquiry, a vision this field shares with others. Among anthropologists in particular, there are also the relationships nurtured through close work with people elsewhere, ties that trail us in and out of campus halls. The strikingly political tone in much of anthropology has something to do with this, with a sense of responsibility for those other relationships and circumstances elsewhere, the various commitments those ties entail. Any tradition of critique, as Mahmood notes, has its own practices of engagement, sociality, and self-cultivation, and its critical capacities owe a great deal to these "cultural, ethical and sensible means."[5] One cannot become an anthropologist without a sense of the critical and transformative force of such implicatedness in the lives of others, because coming of age in the field depends on an exposure to these powers, in the texture of one's own being and beyond.

All the same, it is difficult to remain sanguine now about the forms of experience and exposure that propel anthropological work, most especially with the presumed foundation for such flights into difference, the academic institution. "Our life of the mind has a material basis," Hugh Gusterson recently observed with regard to the United States, "grounded in and paid for by institutions that handle substantial sums of money and play a vital role in mediating the class structure of late capitalism. Over the years," he adds, "almost without our noticing, the institutions in which those conversations take place have become more and more exploitative of those at the bottom of its socioeconomic hierarchies."[6] As public funding for higher education erodes further and further, as students reel under the weight of spiraling debt, as learning is recast as a matter of quantifiable profit and return, and as schools fall back on a precarious labor pool of adjunct instructors for ever more of their basic needs in student teaching and guidance, what remains of that vaunted idea of scholarly critique?

These questions were the focus of a widely circulated online forum, "Academic Precarity in American Anthropology," sponsored by the Society for Cultural Anthropology in the winter of 2018. The authors of the opening essay, David Platzer and Anne Allison—one a graduate student at Johns Hopkins University and the other a senior professor at Duke University—note that "we are driven by passion, an engagement with the world, perhaps even a calling" in moral terms. At the same time, they observe, the acute pressures of the academic labor market had entrenched "anxiety . . . and instability as affects that now defined the experience of graduate school." The tension between these affective registers amounted to a "double bind" in training for careers in anthropology, as if the discipline was asking its apprentice practitioners to commit themselves deeply and truly to a fundamentally impossible life. "How can we be both pragmatic in training students for sustainable jobs and lives," Platzer and Allison ask, "and also visionary in retaining the transformative potential of anthropology as a field?"[7]

It isn't easy, knowing how to face up to this challenge. As all the many contributors to this forum stressed in various ways, these circumstances will demand more openness in how we understand what anthropology and anthropologists can do in the world—giving up, for example, the defensive and demeaning distinction between a properly academic vocation and "applied" work in other domains of practice. Tariq Rahman, a graduate student at the University of California, Irvine, wrote this in response to the opening provocation: "Rather than clinging to a life of the mind that has never been as pure as we make it out to be, our time might be better served by conceptualizing the practice of anthropology otherwise and elsewhere."[8]

Let me admit that I too find myself at a loss when it comes to the scope of these concerns, which verge on questioning the very future of the discipline. One thing that I've learned as an anthropologist, though, is that there are ways of feeling one's way through situations of acute uncertainty, of sifting through the weight of circumstance for elusive yet palpable insight. What remains possible in the idea of the anthropologist as critic? As I have done throughout this book, I want to take up this problem as an ethnographer, to examine what there is, concretely, with an eye to what yet may be. To grasp what is possible with anthropology now, we have to begin with some sense of its contemporary presence, something that it is doing already in the world.

Here, then, is one more story.

IT BEGINS WITH a man trudging slowly down a gravel road, cradling the wounded body of his sister in his arms. Somewhere, we don't know where, things have taken a violent turn. Helicopters hover over the city they have fled, firing into billowing clouds of smoke. She isn't doing well. His eyes are haunted by what they have seen. A voice gently shadows them through abandoned streets, through pine trees and cornfields, through the tattered frame of the tent in which he lays her down at last, giving all of this the semblance of a dark inner vision—

Goldfish-shaped balloons tense
        at coming fire, the sensor
reels and leaves stutter out the window
        of the cell where the translator
peels oranges for the fallen leader.
        The city dims. God
of infinite sets, god of the craters not
        visible to the naked
eye: nothing prepared me for this.
        A man crosses the city,
traveling with his sister to somewhere safe,
        at last the roar paling behind them.
But she falls and cannot walk, so he carries her.
He carries her and carries her until he cannot carry her.
        Then he puts her down.
        He puts her down in the shade.[9]

So it goes with *War Poem*, a short film released by the Minneapolis arts organization Motionpoems in 2018.[10] Like all of their features, the film lends a visual canvas to a contemporary poetic work, one written in this case by the American poet and anthropologist Nomi Stone. This foundation gives *War Poem* its most curious quality, crystallized in the icy blue eyes of the film's protagonist. For Stone's poetry grows out of sustained ethnographic fieldwork in secret places around the United States, where the American military stages simulations of everyday interactions in Iraq for soldiers preparing for deployment. The role-playing exercises rely on the participation of Iraqi refugees, former interpreters now settled in the United States, hired out as mimics of their former selves to give American soldiers a chance to rehearse various scenarios of wartime encounter. This backdrop gives *War Poem* an unsettling edge. Is the film meant to imply that the poem's harrowing vision of wartime Iraq may one day come home to roost in North America? Or are we to take these actors instead as just actors, playing out possible situations of catastrophic loss as exercises in preparedness and mock grief?

"I think the ultimate message to the powers that be," says the director, Ty Richardson, is this: "what if they weren't so distant? How would your own life and circumstance change?"[11]

"Is there a risk here of aesthetics uncoupling from politics?" asks the anthropologist and poet Nomi Stone in return. "We must keep the teeth in politics and remember the very ugly particulars of this country's history, of exactly *who* is suffering and *how*."[12]

Stone has always written poetry alongside her anthropological and ethnographic work. And the relationship between these two modes of expression is especially charged here, for the context is one that instrumentalizes sympathetic affect and empathy. Iraqi players in American war games serve as "human technologies" or affective machines, Stone observes in an incisive article published in *Cultural Anthropology* in 2017. Calling for the performance of anger and grief, "military personnel provide certain parameters for affect, encouraging some affective intensities as registers of the authentic and dissuading others as charged distractions."[13] These exercises also rely on methods essential to anthropology, such as empathetic listening, cultural mimesis, and the search for common humanity, mirroring most darkly what the discipline might be taken to offer the contemporary world: a way to "weaponize new technologies for understanding motivations and patterns of adversaries."[14] What is at stake in casting these grim ambitions in the form of poetry? What kind of critique did such poems afford?

I had the chance to ask Stone these questions in person one afternoon in the fall of 2017. At the time, she was a postdoctoral fellow in anthropology at Princeton University. On the train up from Baltimore, I read slowly through the manuscript of her powerful book of verse based on her fieldwork, *Kill Class*. Reading about the military installations hidden just out of sight beyond the strip malls and motel complexes of everyday America, I couldn't help but imagine their shadows in the trees beside the tracks. "When the wood circles you / back here instead, let the lost / and the impossible ripen / in you, ripen and go," Stone writes in a terse poem that comes late in *Kill Class*. These lines seemed to convey, more acutely than any other, the experience of reading this work: the sense of being encircled and lost within someone else's fable, the promise of something happening but also the uncertainty of what that could be.

We sat for a long chat in her office at Princeton, a stately oak in the window just letting go of its leaves. "Poetry creates a demanding set of conditions for the reader," Nomi admitted, "which can also induce an affective and ethical malaise." This visceral sense of unease, though, also enabled a different mode of critique, one that unfolded "equally well on an affective and embodied register as on a cerebral register." For when it came to circumstances like these simulations, everything turned on the relationship between language and life. Here was a "devastating" situation that ossified words and persons alike, reducing them to objects of manipulation. And all of this was enabled by "the darkest apotheosis of anthropology," where cultural understanding became a tool to identify and neutralize enemies. In the face of such machinations, Nomi suggested, poetry could serve as a way of cracking open rigid pictures of self and other, revealing bewilderment at the heart of certainty, vulnerability where one would expect only hardness, small moments of wonder in the face of horror. "How do you re-embody the word and turn it into a living thing again?" she asked.

We talked about Theodor Adorno, who had declared in 1949 that "to write poetry after Auschwitz is barbaric."[15] This notorious statement is often taken to amount to a blanket condemnation of aesthetic endeavors in the face of annihilating violence. Adorno's own position on the matter though was more complex.[16] "Literature must resist this verdict," he elaborated in 1962, to "be sure that its mere existence after Auschwitz is not a surrender to cynicism."[17] Overtly political and didactic work slid easily into a cultural consecration of pain and atrocity, by drawing such horrors back into circuits of exchange and approbation. Art that did not consciously ally itself with an explicit political outcome, however—the stories of Kafka, say, or the plays of Beckett—still held a different kind of political potential, in the uneasy condition precipitated by their form and structure: the unshakeable sense they gave readers that "it should be otherwise."[18] For Adorno, therefore, everything turned on the possible consequences of experimentation with form. "It is not the office of art to spotlight alternatives," he wrote, "but to resist by its form alone the course of the world."[19] A radical structure of expression could at least gesture toward a possibility that it could not bring about on its own: "the creation of a just life."[20]

I think of the life-and-death struggle at the climax of the title poem in *Kill Class*. Somewhere in the pinelands of North Carolina, she is enlisted to play the role of a guerrilla, Gypsy. She is the only woman among fifty men, and the violence that underlies this fictive scenario quickly becomes too real. She is asked to cry, told of a slain child. Here, now, in the Carolina woods, there is a rabbit that she is told to club and kill. The logic of the simulation is implacable, difficult to evade, and the poem builds to a harrowing scene of the slender young anthropologist encircled by men and by pines, as though caught up in some dark rite of initiation, "the animal screaming," its legs in her arms. Earlier, she says this—

> Sense is an edge, see
>   if you dare   look
>   over into the white
>   falling   We are in
>   a role-play
>   *but if you feel it in there, you feel it.* What is it
>   you think I am lying
>   about, Commander?

Who is this Commander; who is the *I* that is speaking; who is the *you* to whom these words are addressed? That precipitous rim of sense is right there on the page, dropping the reader from person to person, feeling to feeling, inviting a look then catching us up in a whirl of vertiginous possibility. "How do we use form against this, or with it, and through it, and thereby against it?" Nomi asked me, speaking of this military hall of mirrors and her poetry as a mode of response, a way of showing that the reality at stake here was something more than a matter of truth or lie. Could the language broach some kind of real contact that would otherwise be impossible? "I'm staging the set of conditions," she said, "for an otherwise that I would wish to create."

We tend to think of critique as a matter of seeing through things, revealing a hidden and otherwise inaccessible reality, one known only to the critic and made knowable only through the act of critical explanation. To speak of poetry or anthropology as a way to make possible some other way of being and feeling, however, is to invoke a different idea of critique, one that involves the nurturing of openings and possibilities already present in the world and its experience, no matter how dark and desperate those moments may seem.

If you feel it in there, you feel it.

A QUIET SENSE of possibility runs through the difficult scenes of *Kill Class*. It also runs, I would argue, throughout the anthropology present in this book. In all of these essays, the idea has often surfaced of anthropology as a way of tuning into the critical potential of the world at hand, through a certain engagement with experience and its transformative promise. It may rightly be a "dark anthropology" attentive to "the harsh and brutal dimensions of human experience" that predominates in the scholarship of

uneasy times, as Sherry Ortner has put it recently.[21] But we also have enduring resources with which to identify openings for creative engagement with
such circumstances of political violence, economic exploitation, and stark
inequality. That affirmative spirit of critique is what animates this book.

It is there in Bronisław Malinowski's declaration, on the final page of *Argonauts of the Western Pacific*, that "in grasping the essential outlook of others . . . we cannot but help widening our own," and in Zora Neale Hurston's
conviction that even just a portrait of "the average, struggling, non-morbid
Negro" can "do away with that feeling of difference which inspires fear."[22]

It is there in the assertion of Claude Lévi-Strauss that through the study
of a mythic corpus, "the myths criticize and select themselves, opening up"
the path of analysis, and in the commitment of Natasha Myers to a kind of
fieldwork unfolding *alongside* the sentient practices of inquiry pursued by
her arboreal interlocutors.[23]

It is there in Jane Guyer's reliance on open-ended curiosity—"whenever
something is provocative, we pause, and pay attention to it"—as the peda-
gogic foundation of an anthropological classroom, and in Michael Jackson's
sense that writing "allows us to go beyond ourselves, to become other than
what we are or have ever been."[24]

It is there in James Leach's lessons in folded-paper notebooks at a global
conservation conference, everyday means of recording and passing down
indigenous knowledge "without collapsing it into our categories," and in Ursula K. Le Guin's pursuit of ethnography in the form of speculative science
fiction, a way of presenting our era's novel technologies as "weird aberra-
tions" rather than "the only possible reality."[25]

Critique is an art or practice of prising open the fixity of what is present and keeping it open, Michel Foucault argued, "a means for a future or
a truth that it will not know nor happen to be."[26] In this idea of unknown
truths and futures, there is something curious that needs to be unraveled
further. Criticism is typically thought of as a matter of denouncing what is
wrong or unjust, with the idea in mind of a specific alternative, with a notion already of what is right. Indeed, as Raymond Williams notes in *Keywords*, the term "criticism" carries in English "the general sense of fault-
finding, or at least of negative judgment."[27]

To take up critique as a means of tending an open horizon, though, is to
proceed in an affirmative rather than negative manner: to work within the
space of what would seem to be given as a problem in the world, and to seek
out, even here, "a field of possibles, of openings, indecisions, reversals and

possible dislocations."[28] Here is a picture of analysis unfolding in collaboration with potentials already in the world, rather than by stepping aside and pointing out what is absent yet ought to be present. It is a practice infused with existential generosity, with care for what is and its promise of becoming otherwise.[29]

This vision finds its fullest expression in a celebrated interview that Foucault gave to *Le Monde* in 1980, an anonymous exchange we know as "The Masked Philosopher"—

> Judgment is being passed everywhere, all the time. Perhaps it's one of the simplest things mankind has been given to do. And you know very well that the last man, when radiation has finally reduced his last enemy to ashes, will sit down behind some rickety table and begin the trial of the individual responsible. I can't help but dream about a kind of criticism that would try not to judge but to bring an oeuvre, a book, a sentence, an idea to life; it would light fires, watch the grass grow, listen to the wind, and catch the sea foam in the breeze and scatter it. It would multiply not judgments but signs of existence; it would summon them, drag them from their sleep. Perhaps it would invent them sometimes—all the better. All the better. Criticism that hands down sentences sends me to sleep; I'd like a criticism of scintillating leaps of the imagination. It would not be sovereign or dressed in red. It would bear the lightning of possible storms.[30]

These words. Perhaps something happens to you, like me, on reading them. "The mind isn't made of soft wax. It's a reactive substance," Foucault says elsewhere in the interview.[31] And there would appear to be a reason, therefore, for the poetic force gathered into this passage. These words seek to broach a fresh "surface of contact" with the minds of imagined readers, "to land in unexpected places and form shapes," Foucault says, "that I had never thought of."[32] This is critique as an open-ended process of creative emergence. And it is crucial to observe that this is a process understood to begin with empirical encounters, with the "vibrant matter," as Jane Bennett would say, of a living world: fires, grass, wind and foam, books, minds and all.[33]

We in anthropology know this ambition well, we metaphysicians of description. For there is nothing abstract in our critique of humanity; as every ethnography shows, it is by attending to the concrete elements of life, attuning oneself to the critical value of thinking with them, that anthropology opens the horizons of a possible humanity. Like experience, then, the possible has a double life as both object and method in the discipline, both as something to which to turn and consider, and also as the stage of a transformative operation. This is what sustains the field's cosmographic ambition, the aim of reinventing the whole through a shift of perspective, the idea that the world itself can change with the assumption of another point of view.

I could hardly guess who and where you are, as you read these words. But on my desk now, as I bring this manuscript to a close, is the November 2017 issue of *Cultural Anthropology*, published a few days after Nomi and I met in Princeton.[34] On the cover is an image of two young men hanging out with a dog and a bottle of soda in Mexico City, seen through a spiral of barbed-wire fencing. Imagine the journal issue as a kind of time capsule, a momentary portrait of a field. Leafing through the pages within, here is what you'd see.

An anthropologist shows how public education in Los Angeles has come strangely to mirror incarceration; dropping out for black youth is less like failure than escape. A collective of black, brown, and queer women anthropologists recasts fieldwork as violently gendered and embodied trial, seeking after more fugitive prospects of liberatory change. The future in Ghana appears shot through with ruins of the past, tangled unexpectedly with the momentum of long-gone promises and desires. Entanglement itself loses its sheen as critical panacea, taking on the stink of a working-class *colonia* in Mexico City where boundaries have an undeniable value.

A special section on chemical life, in this issue of the journal, aims to unravel "the world as it is but also . . . alter-worlds as they might be."[35] One of its authors invokes the toxic legacies of colonialism, warfare, and industrial pollution that permeate every breath of Toronto's air, daring us to conceive this condition as something other than damage and doom. Another finds the dark outlines of a possible future in a childhood fable, one that is told with fire and flight. "Who will be us," she writes, "is not yet clear," and throughout the issue, this open horizon is what seems to give life to critique.[36]

This book has also presented something like a fable, this possible anthropology: one way of imagining what the field has been, with an eye to what it might offer now and ahead. If there is anything at all that has motivated this effort, it is the problem that propels so much work in the discipline these days, the question of pragmatic value. For we do need ways of seeing the world anew. And stories like ours can be tailored for times of darkness: for moments of profound and unsettling disquiet; in the face of intractable forms of injustice and neglect; as resources for assurance and imagination when the light begins to fade each evening, as it will. We speak into this darkness not with the promise of a dawn to come—who wants to spend all night waiting for that anyway—but instead with the knowledge that the world will feel different when it does.

Like all things, this book grew in company. A few years ago, I began to feel that I needed a better answer to a question that went something like this: *What is anthropology, anyway?* It would come up each semester in classes. People I met in fieldwork would ask this question, as would people whom I met at gatherings back home. In 2010, the discipline gained some notoriety in the United States, when a decision by the executive board of the American Anthropological Association (AAA) to remove the word "science" from the AAA Long-Range Plan somehow became national news. Then too the debates that swirled thereafter seemed caught up in this question: if not a science, then what? I started to follow some of these discussions, and I thought to write an essay of my own in response. But as I began to pursue this question in earnest, it struck me that the answer was not mine alone to give, and that plenty of rich ideas were already around. The idea to pursue this problem as an ethnographer of anthropology made more and more sense. A number of people proved generous enough to allow their own experiences and insights to be folded into the exploration, and a collaborative book project was soon under way.

My first and most fundamental debt is to those colleagues who afforded me glimpses of their own anthropological practice. Jane Guyer and Michael Jackson have been sustaining mentors for many years, while Natasha Myers, Nomi Stone, and Zoe Todd have become inspiring fellow travelers. I am grateful to Monique Lévi-Strauss for her candid reflections, to Frédéric Keck for introducing us, and to both Frédéric and Boris Wiseman for essential insights into Lévi-Strauss the writer. Michael Young took great interest in this project and was kind enough to share drafts of his unpublished biographical work on Bronisław Malinowski—following from the magisterial first volume of his *Malinowski: Odyssey of an Anthropologist*— while Valerie Boyd's extraordinary biography of Zora Neale Hurston was also an essential resource. Richard Lang and Judith Selby Lang invited me with great enthusiasm into their collecting and artistic practice, and Ursula K. Le Guin was kind enough to allow me to examine her letters held in the Special Collections and University Archives of the University of Oregon. This is a book that depends on relations of apprenticeship, and I remain deeply indebted to the lessons of my teachers in anthropology at UC Berkeley—Donald Moore, Lawrence Cohen, Stefania Pandolfo, and Paul Rabinow—to whom this work is dedicated. I wish also to thank the countless other anthropologists from whom I have learned over many years of reading, listening, and thinking alongside, most especially fellow tinkerers of the Society for Cultural Anthropology.

More so than anything else I've written until now, this book developed in an iterative manner, evolving draft by draft through a series of manuscript workshops at the University of Washington, the University of Toronto, UC Berkeley, UC Irvine, and Johns Hopkins University, and talks at Amherst College, George Washington University, Georgetown University, and UCLA. I am profoundly grateful to the organizers and participants in these occasions for close engagement and challenging conversation, most especially Bürge Abiral, Saleem Al-Bahloly, Sareeta Amrute, Alessandro Angelini, Tom Boellstorff, Darren Byler, Frank Cody, Samuele Collu, Veena Das, Naisargi Dave, Michael Degani, Ned Dostaler, Danny Fisher, Camille Frazier, Radhika Govindrajan, Akhil Gupta, Hugh Gusterson, Joshua Griffin, Nathan Hensley, Shweta Krishnan, Adrianna Link, Dana Luciano, Atreyee Majumder, George Marcus, Amira Mittermaier, Fatima Mojaddedi, Keith Murphy, Sumin Myung, Kevin O'Neill, Sherry Ortner, Canay Özden-Schilling, Tom Özden-Schilling, Kris Peterson, Sarah Roth, Peter Skafish, and Sasha Welland. My gratitude is due as well to the students in a few of my seminars at Johns Hopkins—"Encountering Experience," "Ethnography," "The Logic of Anthropology," and "Speculative Anthropology"—where we had the chance to work through these ideas collectively. Evan Kim provided essential assistance with some of this research.

I could not have imagined more thoughtful and insightful reviewers for this manuscript than Stefan Helmreich and a second anonymous reviewer for Duke University Press, and I am thankful for Ken Wissoker's sage counsel and unflagging support. Friends and colleagues who talked through these ideas and read chapter drafts include Nat Adams, Jason Antrosio, Debbora Battaglia, Jane Bennett, Andrew Brandel, Dominic Boyer, Bill Connolly, Alberto Corsín Jiménez, Bob Foster, Angela Garcia, Thalia Gigerenzer, Niloofar Haeri, Clara Han, Tobias Hecht, Cymene Howe, Naveeda Khan, Eben Kirksey, Eduardo Kohn, Jake Kosek, Victor Kumar, Stuart McLean, Tahir Naqvi, Todd Ochoa, David Platzer, Debbie Poole, Lucinda Ramberg, Maya Ratnam, Lisa Stevenson, Robert Thornton, Jason Throop, Gustavo Valdivia, Chitra Venkataramani, and Jarrett Zigon. I am especially grateful to Bob Desjarlais for co-organizing the double session on experience at the 2013 AAA annual meeting, where I first had the chance to float some of the central ideas in this book; to Marisol de la Cadena for the chance to work out some of these ideas in a lively "Methods as Unusual" workshop at UC Davis in 2015; and to Lisa Davis for fishing out, so perceptively, the title for this book from the stream of haphazard verbiage in which it was hidden.

Finally, I'd like to thank my family, Sanchita, Karun, and Uma, for ever offering up the right kind of perspective on that chief vexation of ours in anthropology, humanity. It was Uma who blurted out as a toddler exactly what had to be said one morning when a truck cut us off on the way to her brother's school: "Argh, people!" But she has also promised variously, in the years in which this book was written, to become a butterfly, a tooth fairy, or a purple star when she grows up, and these are some reasons to remain hopeful for the creatures of these times.

INTRODUCTION

1. See Todd, "Should I Stay or Should I Go?"

2. Todd, "Re-situating Alberta as a 'Fish-Place.'"

3. Williams, *Marxism and Literature*, 121–27.

4. Stevenson, *Life beside Itself*, 14.

5. Wagner, *Invention of Culture*, 4.

6. Herder, *Outlines of a Philosophy of the History of Man*, 99.

7. Behar, *Vulnerable Observer*, 14.

8. Tsing, *Mushroom at the End of the World*, 19, 3.

9. Hurston, *Tell My Horse*, 530.

10. Stewart, "Epilogue," in Pandian and McLean, *Crumpled Paper Boat*, 227, 230.

11. Pandian and Mariappan, *Ayya's Accounts*, first published in Tamil as *Mitcham Meethi* in 2012.

12. See Ribeiro, "World Anthropologies," and Boskovic, *Other People's Anthropologies*.

13. Harrison, *Outsider Within*, 8.

14. See Dirks, *Castes of Mind*.

15. Marcus, "Notes toward an Ethnographic Memoir," 27.

16. Forsdick, "*De la plume comme des pieds.*"

17. This project shares in the same spirit of engagement with the history of the discipline as the "joyful history of anthropology" pursued by Bhrigupati Singh and Jane Guyer: "a kind of fullness and intensity of engagement that may include tragic possibilities, and the reemergence of the old as the new, or at least as fodder for the new" ("Joyful History of Anthropology," 201).

18. For a discussion of these ideas, see Pandian, "Time of Anthropology."

19. The subtitle of this introduction gestures toward the classic essay by Bernard S. Cohn, "An Anthropologist among the Historians," put forward as a "field study" that playfully contrasts the ways and views of two different peoples, historians and anthro-

pologists. For an ethnographic perspective on American anthropology, see Ntarangwi, *Reversed Gaze.*

20. See Lévi-Strauss, "Jean-Jacques Rousseau."

21. Sontag, *Against Interpretation.*

22. Ntarangwi, *Reversed Gaze*, 130.

23. I have in mind, among other things, the *Cultural Anthropology* online forum around the essay "Academic Precarity in American Anthropology" by David Platzer and Anne Allison, and the vibrant #hautalk exchanges online precipitated by a spiraling scandal involving the journal *Hau*, most especially Allegra Lab's forum, "Situating #hautalk: A Polyphonic Intervention." Zoe Todd's "The Decolonial Turn 2.0" was a crucial intervention in these debates in the summer of 2018. I also wrote "Open Access, Open Minds," an online reflection for *Cultural Anthropology.*

24. I am grateful to Michael Jackson for this distinction between discipline and profession.

25. Berlant, *Cruel Optimism*, 24.

26. See, respectively, Wilder, "Radical Humanism and Black Atlantic Criticism"; Hayles, *How We Became Posthuman*; and Haraway, *Staying with the Trouble.* See also Connolly, *Facing the Planetary*, for a recent articulation of "entangled humanism" as a critical and political project.

27. I am most grateful to Samuele Collu and Ned Dostaler for organizing this conversation.

28. Foucault, "What Is Enlightenment?," 314.

29. Foucault, "What Is Enlightenment?," 315–16.

30. Foucault, "What Is Enlightenment?," 315.

31. Maniglier, "L'humanisme interminable de Claude Lévi-Strauss," 241.

32. Kozaitis, "Anthropological Praxis in Higher Education," 133, 134.

33. Ginsberg, "Students Look toward the Job Market."

34. Ginsberg, "AAA Members outside the Academy," and Speakman et al., "Market Share and Recent Hiring Trends in Anthropology Faculty Positions."

35. Thanks to Nate Coben for flagging the relevance here of impact factor as criterion.

36. Stein, "Anthropology's 'Impact,'" 13.

37. Fassin, "Introduction," 8.

38. Garcia, *Pastoral Clinic*, 35.

39. Povinelli, "Will to Be Otherwise," 472, 453.

Chapter One. THE WORLD AT HAND

1. Malinowski, *Freedom and Civilization*, 312.

2. Malinowski, *Freedom and Civilization*, 213.

3. Malinowski, *Freedom and Civilization*, 3.

4. Malinowski, *Freedom and Civilization*, 43.

5. Hurston, *Dust Tracks on a Road*, 793.

6. Hurston, *Dust Tracks on a Road*, 789-90.

7. Ingold, *Being Alive*, 241–42, 238. There were many philosophers who were known to do just this. Take Henry David Thoreau, who advised in "Walking" that "you must walk like a camel, which is said to be the only beast which ruminates when walking" (601). Or Friedrich Nietzsche, who penned these lines into *The Gay Science*: "We do not belong to those who have ideas only among books, when stimulated by books. It is our habit to think outdoors—walking, leaping, climbing, dancing, preferably on lonely mountains or near the sea where even the trails become thoughtful" (322).

8. Jackson, *Paths toward a Clearing*, 182.

9. While I share William Mazzarella's interest in "how emergent concerns in the present might activate hitherto unrealized potentials in the mimetic archive of the discipline" (*Mana of Mass Society*, 12), my evaluation here of early empiricist legacies in the discipline differs from his. The "empiricist settlement," as he puts it, remained unsettled by the force of such expressive powers, as seen in the affinity of the scientific and literary.

10. Downie, *James George Frazer*, 100.

11. Malinowski, *Myth in Primitive Psychology*, 16–17.

12. Kuklick, "Personal Equations."

13. Freire-Marreco and Myres, *Notes and Queries*, 110.

14. Stocking, "Ethnographer's Magic," 109.

15. Malinowski, "Baloma," 353–54.

16. Malinowski, "Baloma," 421.

17. Malinowski, "Baloma," 419.

18. Malinowski, "Baloma," 418.

19. Malinowski, "Baloma," 411.

20. Malinowski, "Baloma," 369.

21. Malinowski, "Baloma," 417.

22. See Delaney, "Meaning of Paternity and the Virgin Birth Debate."

23. Malinowski, "Baloma," 421.

24. Malinowski, "Baloma," 429.

25. Malinowski, "Baloma," 419.

26. Malinowski, "Baloma," 419.

27. Malinowski, "Baloma," 415.

28. This idea, of great interest in contemporary anthropology and other disciplines—see, for example, Jensen, "Continuous Variations," and Zhan, "Empirical as Conceptual"—owes an important intellectual debt to Melanesian anthropology. Take, for example, not only Malinowski but Marilyn Strathern's *Gender of the Gift*, which endeavored "to show the contextualized nature of indigenous constructs by exposing the contextualized nature of analytical ones," such that "the analytical constructs themselves [are] located in the society that produced them" (8).

29. Young, *Malinowski*, chapter 20.

30. Malinowski, *Diary in the Strict Sense of the Term*, 255.

31. Wayne, *Story of a Marriage*, 111.

32. Wayne, *Story of a Marriage*, 112.

33. Malinowski, *Argonauts of the Western Pacific*, 25.

34. Malinowski, *Diary in the Strict Sense of the Term*, 119.

35. Malinowski, "Baloma," 417.

36. Robeson, *African Journey*, 14–15.

37. Boyd, *Wrapped in Rainbows*.

38. Hurston, *Dust Tracks on a Road*, 122.

39. Boyd, *Wrapped in Rainbows*, 251–52.

40. Hurston, *Dust Tracks on a Road*, 123.

41. Hurston, *Dust Tracks on a Road*, 128.

42. Franz Boas to Zora Neale Hurston, letter dated May 3, 1927, in *Professional Correspondence of Franz Boas*.

43. Mead, "Apprenticeship under Boas," 29.

44. Boas to Hurston, letter dated May 3, 1927, in *Professional Correspondence of Franz Boas*.

45. Kaplan, *Zora Neale Hurston*, 138.

46. Kaplan, *Zora Neale Hurston*, 115–16.

47. Boyd, *Wrapped in Rainbows*, 436.

48. Boyd, *Wrapped in Rainbows*, 252.

49. Clifford, *Predicament of Culture*, 34.

50. Strathern, "Out of Context," 254.

51. Hurston, *Mules and Men*, xiii.

52. Hurston, *Mules and Men*, 1. For a discussion about the politics of this metaphor for the anthropological vantage point, see Jacobs, "From 'Spy-Glass' to 'Horizon.'"

53. Hurston, *Mules and Men*, 121.

54. Hurston, *Mules and Men*, 164.

55. Hurston, *Mules and Men*, 221.

56. Hurston, *Mules and Men*, 246.

57. "She demands that we become more attuned to both the polyphony and cacophony resounding in the world around us and that we commit ourselves to the call of those voices," Graciela Hernandez observes of Hurston in "Multiple Subjectivities and Strategic Positionality," 162.

58. Kaplan, *Zora Neale Hurston*, 308.

59. Wagner, *Anthropology of the Subject*, 15–16.

60. Wagner, *Anthropology of the Subject*, 17.

61. Hurston, "What White Publishers Won't Print," 950.

62. Hurston, "What White Publishers Won't Print," 951–52.

63. Kaplan, *Zora Neale Hurston*, 286.

64. Hurston, *Mules and Men*, 120.

65. Malinowski, *Argonauts of the Western Pacific*, 267.

66. Malinowski, *Diary in the Strict Sense of the Term*, 236.

67. E. Leach, "Epistemological Background to Malinowski's Empiricism," 120.

68. Banks, *Realistic Empiricism of Mach, James, and Russell*.

69. Mach, *Knowledge and Error*, 361.

70. Mach, *Popular Scientific Lectures*, 190.

71. Malinowski, "On the Principle of the Economy of Thought," 115.

72. Malinowski, *Diary in the Strict Sense of the Term*, 253.

73. Malinowski, *Diary in the Strict Sense of the Term*, 132.

74. Malinowski, *Diary in the Strict Sense of the Term*, 253.

75. Malinowski, *Diary in the Strict Sense of the Term*, 236.

76. Clifford, "On Ethnographic Self-Fashioning," in Clifford, *Predicament of Culture*.

77. Malinowski, *Diary in the Strict Sense of the Term*, 247.

78. Young, *Malinowski*, 88–90.

79. Malinowski (Bronisław) Papers, MS 19, Series II, Box 27, Folder 239, Yale University Library.

80. Hurston, *Tell My Horse*, 383.

81. Hurston, *Tell My Horse*, 387.

82. Hurston, *Tell My Horse*, 393.

83. Gates, "Negro Way of Saying."

84. Crapanzano, *Imaginative Horizons*, 14.

85. Kaplan, *Zora Neale Hurston*, 286.

86. Malinowski, *Argonauts of the Western Pacific*, 298.

87. Malinowski, *Myth in Primitive Psychology*, 18–19.

88. Malinowski, *Myth in Primitive Psychology*, 13.

89. Malinowski, *Myth in Primitive Psychology*, 81.

90. Malinowski, *Myth in Primitive Psychology*, 57.

91. Malinowski, *Diary in the Strict Sense of the Term*, 35.

92. Malinowski, *Diary in the Strict Sense of the Term*, 98.

93. Malinowski, *Diary in the Strict Sense of the Term*, 157.

94. Malinowski, *Diary in the Strict Sense of the Term*, 178.

95. Malinowski, *Diary in the Strict Sense of the Term*, 54.

96. See Young's discussion of "the turmoil of letters" in *Malinowski*, 520–26.

97. Wayne, *Story of a Marriage*, 81.

98. Marcus, "Notes toward an Ethnographic Memoir."

99. Malinowski, *Argonauts of the Western Pacific*, 237.

100. Throughout this essay, my understanding of Malinowski's intentions and interior life has been deeply indebted to the biographical work of Michael Young, who was kind enough to supplement the published first volume of *Malinowski: Odyssey of an Anthropologist, 1884–1920* with unpublished chapters of a second volume that he shared with me, pages that describe, for example, debates and deliberations over the proper titling of this book.

101. Malinowski, *Coral Gardens*, vol. 1, 1.

102. Geertz, *Works and Lives*.

103. Malinowski, *Coral Gardens*, vol. 1, 4.

104. Malinowski, *Argonauts of the Western Pacific*, 6.

105. Taussig, *What Color Is the Sacred?*, 83.

106. Malinowski, *Coral Gardens*, vol. 2, 9.

107. Malinowski, *Coral Gardens*, vol. 2, 240–41.

108. James, *Essays in Radical Empiricism*.

109. Malinowski (Bronisław) Papers, MS 19, Series II, Box 27, Folder 239, Yale University Library. For an illuminating discussion, see Young, Malinowski, 82–90.

110. Malinowski, *Coral Gardens*, vol. 2, 215.

111. Malinowski, *Coral Gardens*, vol. 2, 70.

112. Malinowski, *Diary in the Strict Sense of the Term*, 17.

113. Malinowski, *Coral Gardens*, vol. 2, 229.

114. Malinowski, *Coral Gardens*, vol. 2, 58.

115. Malinowski, *Magic, Science, and Religion*, 70.

116. Hurston, *Their Eyes Were Watching God*, 51.

117. Hurston, *Their Eyes Were Watching God*, 48.

118. Hurston, *Their Eyes Were Watching God*, 183.

119. Hurston, *Their Eyes Were Watching God*, 10, 7.

120. Hurston, *Their Eyes Were Watching God*, 182.

121. Anthropology is "embedded within its own regime of enchantment," Graham Jones argues in *Magic's Reason*, "something like a web of affect-laden agreements about how forms of human and non-human agency are distributed and interrelated within cosmological and/or sociopolitical systems" (163).

122. Hurston, *Mules and Men*, 183.

123. Hurston, *Their Eyes Were Watching God*, 184.

124. For more on this way of thinking of ethnographic writing, see Pandian and McLean, *Crumpled Paper Boat*.

125. Hurston, *Dust Tracks on a Road*, 687.

126. Hurston, *Dust Tracks on a Road*, 690–91.

127. Hurston, *Dust Tracks on a Road*, 691.

128. Hurston, *Dust Tracks on a Road*, 687.

129. Hurston, *Dust Tracks on a Road*, 695.

130. Boas, "Study of Geography," 645.

131. Boas, "Study of Geography," 642.

132. Deleuze, *Difference and Repetition*, xix, 176.

133. Malinowski, *Diary in the Strict Sense of the Term*, 219.

134. Kaplan, *Zora Neale Hurston*, 376.

135. Hurston, *Barracoon*, 57.

136. Hurston, *Barracoon*, 93.

137. "Potentiality as an analytic implies working from a classic anthropological awareness that things could be other than they are" (K. Taussig, Hoeyer, and Helmreich, "Anthropology of Potentiality in Biomedicine," 56).

Chapter Two. A METHOD OF EXPERIENCE

1. Daniel, *Charred Lullabies*, 3.

2. Raheja and Gold, *Listen to the Heron's Words*, xxv–xxvi.

3. Cohen, *No Aging in India*, 35, 37.

4. Daniel, *Charred Lullabies*, 6.

5. Daniel, *Charred Lullabies*, 153, quoting Emily Dickinson.

6. Wolf, *Anthropology*, 88.

7. Geertz, *Works and Lives*, 10.

8. Evans-Pritchard, "Appendix IV: Some Reminiscences and Reflections on Field-work," in *Witchcraft, Oracles and Magic among the Azande*, 241.

9. For Western explorers in the colonial era, Sawyer and Agrawal observe in "Environmental Orientalisms," a tropics conceived as essentially feminine by nature held "the promise of passion and peril" (75).

10. Daston and Galison, *Objectivity*, 199.

11. Turner, "Experience and Performance," 226.

12. Clifford, *Predicament of Culture*, 35, 37.

13. Scott, "Evidence of Experience."

14. Clifford, *Predicament of Culture*, 37.

15. Dilthey, "The Construction of the Historical World in the Human Studies," in *Selected Writings*, 176.

16. Jay, *Songs of Experience*, 405.

17. Williams, *Keywords*, 116.

18. Rheinberger, "Art of Exploring the Unknown," 143.

19. Ethnography is a "way of staying connected to open-ended, even mysterious, social processes and uncertainties—a way of counterbalancing the generation of certainties and foreclosures by other disciplines," João Biehl observes in "Ethnography in the Way of Theory," 590.

20. Tyler, "Post-modern Ethnography," 138.

21. Desjarlais and Throop, "Phenomenological Approaches in Anthropology," 93.

22. Viveiros de Castro, "Zeno and the Art of Anthropology," 138.

23. Wilcken, *Claude Lévi-Strauss*, 111.

24. Boyarin, *Ethnography of Reading*.

25. Turner, "Experience and Performance," 209, 210.

26. Lévi-Strauss, *Naked Man*, 632. A singular guide to questions of method in Lévi-Strauss may be found in Boris Wiseman's *Lévi-Strauss, Anthropology, and Aesthetics*, which takes up this passage as an example of the importance of unconscious suggestion for Lévi-Strauss.

27. Quoted in and translated by Wiseman, *Lévi-Strauss, Anthropology, and Aesthetics*, 200.

28. Wiseman, *Lévi-Strauss, Anthropology, and Aesthetics*, 200.

29. Lévi-Strauss, *Raw and the Cooked*, 15.

30. Lévi-Strauss, *Raw and the Cooked*, 31–32.

31. Lévi-Strauss, "From Chrétien de Troyes to Richard Wagner," in *View from Afar*, 219.

32. Lévi-Strauss, *Raw and the Cooked*, 6.

33. Lévi-Strauss, "From Chrétien de Troyes to Richard Wagner," 232.

34. Lévi-Strauss, *Raw and the Cooked*, 118, 286.

35. Whittall, "Music," 64.

36. Lévi-Strauss, *Raw and the Cooked*, 17.

37. Debaene, *Far Afield*, x.

38. Lévi-Strauss, *Tristes Tropiques*, 53.

39. Clifford, *Routes*, 65.

40. A wonderful volume in this regard is Narayan, *Alive in the Writing*.

41. On the vicissitudes of the writing process in anthropology, see "Archipelagoes: A Voyage in Writing," by the Paper Boat Collective, in Pandian and McLean, *Crumpled Paper Boat*.

42. Jackson, *Other Shore*, 22.

43. Jackson, *Other Shore*, 172.

44. Forsdick, "De la plume comme des pieds."

45. Jackson, *Other Shore*, 3.

46. Guyer, "'Quickening of the Unknown,'" 289.

47. Guyer, "'Quickening of the Unknown,'" 287.

48. Guyer, "'Quickening of the Unknown,'" 288.

49. Guyer, "'Quickening of the Unknown,'" 286.

50. Verran, "Staying True to the Laughter," 151.

51. For a discussion of this image, see Draaisma, "Memoria: Memory as Writing," in *Metaphors of Memory*.

52. "The notion that an artistic or intellectual work can start from elements and yet avoid being essentialist or reductive echoes my own provisional fixing of a conceptual starting point that would be amplified, contextualized, and thereby altered as the work developed" (Guyer, *Marginal Gains*, 24).

53. Rancière, *Ignorant Schoolmaster*, 21.

54. Rancière, *Ignorant Schoolmaster*, 29–30.

55. Kant, *Anthropology from a Pragmatic Point of View*, 160.

56. Kant, *Anthropology from a Pragmatic Point of View*, 150.

57. Kant, *Anthropology from a Pragmatic Point of View*, 20.

58. da Col, "Strathern Bottle," xiii.

59. Powdermaker, *Stranger and Friend*, 35.

60. Guyer, "'Quickening of the Unknown,'" 298.

61. Shore, "Fictions of Fieldwork," 33.

62. See Hoffmann, "Unity of Science and Art."

63. Myers, *Rendering Life Molecular*, 72–73.

64. Hustak and Myers, "Involutionary Momentum."

65. Myers, *Rendering Life Molecular*, 238.

66. Myers, "Conversations on Plant Sensing."

67. Daston, "On Scientific Observation," 107.

68. Mead, *Blackberry Winter*, 142.

69. "We have seen in this report that there are real and present dangers associated with fieldwork," Nancy Howell concludes in her 1990 survey for the American Anthropological Association Advisory Panel on Health and Safety in Fieldwork (*Surviving Fieldwork*, 182).

70. For a powerful account of gender violence, and embodied experience more generally, as impetus for women anthropologists of color "to research and write from places of positioned truth," see Berry et al., "Toward a Fugitive Anthropology."

71. Rosaldo, "The Fly," in *Day of Shelly's Death*, 67.

72. Rosaldo, "Grief and a Headhunter's Rage," in *Day of Shelly's Death*, 123.

73. Rosaldo, *Day of Shelly's Death*, 105.

74. Gupta and Ferguson, "Discipline and Practice," 37.

75. James, *Essays in Radical Empiricism*, 71.

76. Dewey, *Art as Experience*, 38.

77. Jackson, *Accidental Anthropologist*, 266.

78. Jackson, *Accidental Anthropologist*, 312.

79. Carlson, "Precarious Love."

80. Foucault, "Interview with Michel Foucault," 242.

81. See Raffles, "Twenty-Five Years Is a Long Time," on the prospect of an "ethnography of stone."

Chapter Three. FOR THE HUMANITY YET TO COME

1. Latour, "Anthropology at the Time of the Anthropocene."

2. Chakrabarty, "Climate of History," 222.

3. Malm and Hornborg, "Geology of Mankind."

4. Kirksey and Helmreich, "Emergence of Multispecies Ethnography," 566.

5. Tsing, "More-Than-Human Sociality," 33.

6. Sagan, "Human Is More than Human."

7. Kohn, *How Forests Think*, 42.

8. Kohn, *How Forests Think*, 134.

9. Kohn, *How Forests Think*, 133.

10. Carrithers, "Anthropology as a Moral Science of Possibilities," 434.

11. Haraway, *Staying with the Trouble*, 103. "Kin is a wild category that all sorts of people do their best to domesticate," she observes elsewhere in the book. "Making kin as oddkin rather than, or at least in addition to, godkin and genealogical and biogenetic family troubles important matters, like to whom one is actually responsible" (2).

12. I ought to acknowledge that this position is different from the one that Haraway takes in *Staying with the Trouble*, in proposing, for example, Chthulucene as an alternative to Anthropocene. "There are so many kin who might better have named this time of the Anthropocene that is at stake now," Haraway writes. "The anthropos is too much of a parochial fellow; he is both too big and too small for most of the needed stories" (174). My effort in the present essay is to try to suggest that *anthropos* remains a being of indeterminate shape and nature, and that there remains a value, therefore, in staying with the trouble of this particular being.

13. Feldman and Ticktin, "Government and Humanity," 25.

14. Fassin, "Inequality of Lives, Hierarchies of Humanity," 239.

15. Descola, *Beyond Nature and Culture*, 191.

16. Descola, *Beyond Nature and Culture*, 177.

17. Descola, *Beyond Nature and Culture*, 81. Eduardo Viveiros de Castro similarly describes "the nature/culture distinction" as "that first article of the Constitution of an-

thropology, whereby it pledges allegiance to the ancient matrix of Western metaphysics" (*Cannibal Metaphysics*, 55).

18. Descola, *Beyond Nature and Culture*, xx.

19. Descola, *Beyond Nature and Culture*, 11.

20. Bunzl, "Franz Boas and the Humboldtian Tradition"; Forster, "Herder and the Birth of Modern Anthropology"; Zammito, *Kant, Herder, and the Birth of Anthropology*.

21. Herder, *Philosophical Writings*, 395.

22. Zammito, "Epigenesis," 137.

23. Zammito, "Epigenesis," 137.

24. Herder, *Outlines*, 99.

25. Herder, *Outlines*, 99–100.

26. Herder, *Philosophical Writings*, 336.

27. Herder, *Philosophical Writings*, 292; Sikka, *Herder on Humanity and Cultural Difference*, 249.

28. Herder, *On World History*, 193.

29. Herder, *Philosophical Writings*, 394–95.

30. "All humans move toward what might be considered an ideal humanity by cultivating and exercising their powers in manifold ways," Sankar Muthu observes of Herder's thought in *Enlightenment against Empire*, 235.

31. Herder, *Philosophical Writings*, 382.

32. Multiculturalism, therefore, does not necessarily imply mononaturalism, as Viveiros de Castro argues in *Cannibal Metaphysics*.

33. Herder, *Philosophical Writings*, 395.

34. See Sikka, "The Question of Moral Relativism," in *Herder on Humanity and Cultural Difference*.

35. Herder, *Outlines*, 201.

36. Herder, *Philosophical Writings*, 396–97.

37. Forster, "Herder and the Birth of Modern Anthropology."

38. Boas, "Anthropologist's Credo," 202–3.

39. See Cole, *Franz Boas*, 261–75.

40. Boas, "Aims of Ethnology," 636.

41. Price, *Cold War Anthropology*.

42. Rabinow, *Anthropos Today*, 6.

43. James, *Pragmatism*, 46–47.

44. Bateson, *Steps toward an Ecology of Mind*, 315. Recall also what William James suggested in his lectures in *Pragmatism*: "There can be no difference anywhere that doesn't make a difference elsewhere—no difference in abstract truth that doesn't express itself in a difference in concrete fact and in conduct consequent upon that fact, imposed on somebody, somehow, somewhere, and somewhen. The whole function of philosophy ought to be to find out what definite difference it would make to you and me, at definite instants of our life, if this world-formula or that world-formula be the true one" (49–50).

45. Peluso, "Coercing Conservation?"

46. UNEP-WCMC and IUCN, *Protected Planet Report 2016*, 39.

47. Strathern, "No Nature, No Culture," 181. See also West, *Conservation Is Our Government Now*; Walley, *Rough Waters*; and Helmreich, "Nature/Culture/Seawater."

48. Stengers, "Cosmopolitical Proposal," 996.

49. "*Kawsak Sacha*—Living Forest," Pueblo Originario Kichwa de Sarayaku. For a discussion of this proposal, see Kohn, "Ecopolitics."

50. To attend to these anthropological inflections in a space like the World Conservation Congress is not just to provide a different perspective on a single event, but instead, as Strathern herself suggests in *Partial Connections*, "to make it evident that, as a constellation of elements, each position generates a further elaboration with an enlarging and diminishing effect on the constellations of the previous position" (108). Perspectives here, in other words, were active and dynamic forces of organization, changing the nature of what unfolded as they were assumed.

51. "New Coalition Launches to Scale Private Conservation Investment at IUCN World Conservation Congress," IUCN press release, September 2, 2016.

52. During the conference itself, Samuels published online a trenchant critique of the "ideological conflict" at stake in the IUCN's difficulty with indigenous perspectives on conservation and the natural world, arguing that "in indigenous cultures and beliefs, nature herself is human whereas the western concept of conservation seeks to divorce the human element from landscape." See Samuels, "Global Conservation Problem Is in the Photos."

53. In this sense, the 2016 WCC appears to have been rather different, in my experience, from the very circumscribed role for critical social science perspectives that Welch-Devine and Campbell, "Sorting Out Roles and Defining Divides," report for the 2008 WCC in Barcelona.

54. On the Rai coast of Papua New Guinea, James Leach observes in *Creative Land* that "knowledge of the land is not generated and mediated through representations, but through the work of generating other people" (207).

55. Tumarkin, "Miklouho-Maclay," 5.

56. Stengers, "Cosmopolitical Proposal," 995.

57. Richard Lang and Judith Selby Lang, *The Plasticene Discontinuity*, San Francisco Bay Model Visitor Center, Sausalito, CA, November 1—December 27, 2004. This exhibition booklet was shared by the artists with the author in 2016.

58. Zalasiewicz et al., "Geological Cycle of Plastics."

59. See, for example, Longobardi, *Drifters*, and Davis and Turpin, *Art in the Anthropocene*.

60. Schneider and Wright, "Challenge of Practice," 15.

61. Foster, "Artist as Ethnographer?," 305.

62. For the exhibition catalogue and essays, see Decker, *Gyre*.

63. Miner, "Body Ritual among the Nacirema."

64. Dewey, *Art as Experience*, 109.

65. Ursula K. Le Guin Papers, Correspondence, Subseries D, Coll 270, Box 16, Folder 15, Special Collections and University Archives, University of Oregon Library.

66. Le Guin, *Language of the Night*, 145.

67. Le Guin, *Left Hand of Darkness*, 59, 71.

68. Ursula K. Le Guin Papers, Correspondence, Subseries D, Coll 270, Box 16, Folder 5, Special Collections and University Archives, University of Oregon Library.

69. Ursula K. Le Guin Papers, Correspondence, Subseries D, Coll 270, Box 45, Folder 16, Special Collections and University Archives, University of Oregon Library. Italics added.

70. Quoted in Baker-Cristales, "Poiesis of Possibility," 23–24.

71. Le Guin, *Wave in the Mind*, 14, 15.

72. Kroeber, *Ishi in Two Worlds*.

73. Le Guin, *Dispossessed*, 208.

74. Le Guin, *Telling*, 95.

75. Le Guin, *Wave in the Mind*, 29.

76. Le Guin, *Wave in the Mind*, 30.

77. Le Guin, *Left Hand of Darkness*, 100.

78. Le Guin, *Left Hand of Darkness*, 232, 33.

79. Le Guin, *Left Hand of Darkness*, 296.

80. Wagner, *Invention of Culture*, 12.

81. Viveiros de Castro, *Cannibal Metaphysics*, 196.

82. For an invigorating account of anthropology as an "art of fabulation" that lends itself to "a project of ontological *poeisis* rather than one of comparative ontology," see McLean, *Fictionalizing Anthropology*, 95, 85.

83. Jackson, *Conversations with Ursula K. Le Guin*, 27.

84. Latour, *Inquiry into Modes of Existence*, 242.

85. Dillon, *Walking the Clouds*.

86. Le Guin, *Worlds of Exile and Illusion*, 281.

87. Le Guin, *Worlds of Exile and Illusion*, 362, 281.

88. Le Guin, *Worlds of Exile and Illusion*, 363.

89. Scranton, *Learning to Die in the Anthropocene*, 14, 22.

90. Scranton, *Learning to Die in the Anthropocene*, 19.

91. Fischer, *Anthropological Futures*, 3.

92. I am grateful to Bürge for her many insights into the arguments of this essay.

93. Tsing, *Mushroom at the End of the World*, 137.

94. Reno, *Waste Away*, 2, 5.

95. Myers, *Rendering Life Molecular*, 99, 100.

96. Pandian, *Reel World*, 4.

97. De León, *Land of Open Graves*, 253, 261.

98. Stevenson, *Life Beside Itself*, 140.

99. Stevenson, *Life Beside Itself*, 86.

100. Deleuze and Guattari, *What Is Philosophy?*, 109.

101. Deleuze, *Cinema 2*, 221–22.

102. Markus, "Culture."

103. Denby, "Herder," 67; "Culture," in Williams, *Keywords*.

104. "How Philosophy Can Become More Universal and Useful for the Benefit of the People," in Herder, *Philosophical Writings*, 8.

105. "On the Change of Taste," in Herder, *Philosophical Writings*, 249.

106. Césaire, *Discourse on Colonialism*, 41, 73.

107. Césaire, *Journal of a Homecoming*, 117. "Césaire's assertion of a common human-ity relies not on some notion of resemblance or shared experience, but on an under-standing of the need for an ethical relation with the other as other," Jane Hiddleston writes in "Aimé Césaire and Postcolonial Humanism," 88. See also Kullberg, *Poetics of Ethnography in Martinican Narratives*, which shows how "Martinican authors appropri-ate and transform ethnography, distorting it into a poetics in order to explore the self in relation to the Caribbean's cyclonic reality" (9).

108. Césaire, *Journal of a Homecoming*, 93.

CODA

1. Price, "One Who Raged against the Machine."

2. Berreman, "'Bringing It All Back Home,'" 90.

3. Scheper-Hughes, "Primacy of the Ethical," 420, 431.

4. Mahmood, "Religious Reason and Secular Affect: An Incommensurable Divide?," in Asad et al., *Is Critique Secular?*, 85.

5. Mahmood, "Reply to Judith Butler," in Asad et al., *Is Critique Secular?*, 153.

6. Gusterson, "Homework," 443.

7. Platzer and Allison, "Academic Precarity in American Anthropology."

8. Rahman, "Precarity of Academic Work, the Work of Academic Precarity."

9. Nomi Stone, "War Poem," *New Republic*, May 2, 2017.

10. The film is available to see at http://motionpoems.org/episode/war-poem/.

11. "Experience the Refugee Journey through Western Eyes in Ty Richardson's Emotive Short 'War Poem,'" June 19, 2018, https://directorsnotes.com/2018/06/19/ty-richardson-war-poem/.

12. Stone, "Aesthetics and Politics."

13. Stone, "Living the Laughscream," 162.

14. Stone, "Living the Laughscream," 151.

15. Adorno, "Cultural Criticism and Society," 33.

16. For an illuminating discussion, see Zilcosky, "Poetry after Auschwitz?"

17. Adorno, "Commitment," 84.

18. Adorno, "Commitment," 89.

19. Adorno, "Commitment," 78.

20. Adorno, "Commitment," 89. On the politics of form, see also Mitchell, "Com-mitment to Form."

21. Ortner, "Dark Anthropology and Its Others," 49.

22. Malinowski, *Argonauts*, 518; Hurston, "What White Publishers Won't Print," 954.

23. Lévi-Strauss, *Naked Man*, 632.

24. Jackson, *Other Shore*, 93.

25. Freedman, *Conversations with Ursula K. Le Guin*, 102.

26. Foucault, "What Is Critique?," 41.

27. Williams, *Keywords*, 85.

28. The phrase is from Foucault, "What Is Critique?," 66. See also Massumi, "On Critique," for more about affirmative and negative modes of critique.

29. As William E. Connolly writes in *The Fragility of Things*, "an ethos exuding existential gratitude, amid the vitality and vulnerabilities that mark life, can . . . help to mobilize surplus energies needed to work experimentally upon the institutional roles that now help to situate us culturally . . . to renegotiate the modes of political activism in play today" (181).

30. Foucault, "Masked Philosopher," 323.

31. Foucault, "Masked Philosopher," 325.

32. Foucault, "Masked Philosopher," 321. Hence the anonymity of the interview.

33. Bennett, *Vibrant Matter*. See also "An Anthropology of Creation" in Pandian, *Reel World*.

34. Although the journal went largely virtual with the transition to open-access publishing, print subscriptions remain available and help to sustain this uncommon enterprise.

35. Shapiro and Kirksey, "Chemo-Ethnography," 487.

36. Povinelli, "Fires, Fogs, Winds," 512.

Adorno, Theodor. "Commitment." *New Left Review I*, no. 87–88 (1974): 75–89.

Adorno, Theodor. "Cultural Criticism and Society." In *Prisms*, translated by Samuel and Shierry Weber, 17–33. Cambridge, MA: MIT Press, 1981.

Allegra Lab. "Situating #hautalk: A Polyphonic Intervention." June 19, 2018. http:// allegralaboratory.net/situating-hautalk-a-polyphonic-intervention/.

Asad, Talal, Wendy Brown, Judith Butler, and Saba Mahmood. *Is Critique Secular? Blasphemy, Injury, and Free Speech*. New York: Fordham University Press, 2013.

Baker-Cristales, Beth. "Poiesis of Possibility: The Ethnographic Sensibilities of Ursula K. Le Guin." *Anthropology and Humanism* 37, no. 1 (2012): 15–26.

Banks, Erik. *The Realistic Empiricism of Mach, James, and Russell: Neutral Monism Reconceived*. Cambridge: Cambridge University Press, 2014.

Bateson, Gregory. *Steps toward an Ecology of Mind*. Chicago: University of Chicago Press, 2000.

Behar, Ruth. *The Vulnerable Observer: Anthropology That Breaks Your Heart*. Boston: Beacon, 1996.

Bennett, Jane. *Vibrant Matter: A Political Ecology of Things*. Durham, NC: Duke University Press, 2010.

Berlant, Lauren. *Cruel Optimism*. Durham, NC: Duke University Press, 2011.

Berreman, Gerald. "'Bringing It All Back Home': Malaise in Anthropology." In *Reinventing Anthropology*, edited by Dell Hymes, 83–98. New York: Pantheon, 1972.

Berry, Maya J., Claudia Chavez Arguelles, Shanya Cordis, Sarah Ihmoud, and Elizabeth Velasquez Estrada. "Toward a Fugitive Anthropology: Gender, Race, and Violence in the Field." *Cultural Anthropology* 32, no. 4 (2017): 537–65.

Biehl, João. "Ethnography in the Way of Theory." *Cultural Anthropology* 28, no. 4 (2013): 573–97.

Boas, Franz. "The Aims of Ethnology." In *A Race, Language, and Culture*, 626–38. New York: Macmillan, 1940.

Boas, Franz. "An Anthropologist's Credo." *The Nation* 147, no. 6 (1938): 201–4.

Boas, Franz. *Professional Correspondence of Franz Boas.* Wilmington: Scholarly Resources, 1972.

Boas, Franz. "The Study of Geography." In *Race, Language, and Culture,* 639–47. New York: Macmillan, 1940.

Boskovic, Aleksandar. *Other People's Anthropologies: Ethnographic Practice on the Margins.* New York: Berghahn, 2008.

Boyarin, Jonathan. *The Ethnography of Reading.* Berkeley: University of California Press, 1993.

Boyd, Valerie. *Wrapped in Rainbows: The Life of Zora Neale Hurston.* New York: Scribner, 2004.

Bunzl, Matti. "Franz Boas and the Humboldtian Tradition: From *Volksgeist* and *Nationalcharakter* to an Anthropological Concept of Culture." In *Volksgeist as Method and Ethic: Essays on Boasian Ethnography and the German Anthropological Tradition,* edited by George Stocking, 17–78. Madison: University of Wisconsin Press, 1996.

Carlson, Jennifer. "Precarious Love: On Solidarity in Times of Collapse." Dialogues, *Cultural Anthropology* website, February 12, 2018. https://culanth.org/fieldsights /1312-precarious-love-on-solidarity-in-times-of-collapse.

Carrithers, Michael. "Anthropology as a Moral Science of Possibilities." *Current Anthropology* 46, no. 3 (2005): 433–56.

Césaire, Aimé. *Discourse on Colonialism.* Translated by Joan Pinkham. New York: Monthly Review Press, 2000.

Césaire, Aimé. *Journal of a Homecoming.* Translated by N. Gregson Davis. Durham, NC: Duke University Press, 2017.

Chakrabarty, Dipesh. "The Climate of History: Four Theses." *Critical Inquiry* 35, no. 2 (2009): 197–222.

Clifford, James. *The Predicament of Culture.* Cambridge, MA: Harvard University Press, 1988.

Clifford, James. *Routes: Travel and Translation in the Late Twentieth Century.* Cambridge, MA: Harvard University Press, 1997.

Cohen, Lawrence. *No Aging in India: Alzheimer's, the Bad Family, and Other Modern Things.* Berkeley: University of California Press, 1998.

Cohn, Bernard S. "An Anthropologist among the Historians: A Field Study." In *An Anthropologist among the Historians and Other Essays,* 1–17. Delhi: Oxford University Press, 1987.

Cole, Douglas. *Franz Boas: The Early Years, 1859–1906.* Seattle: University of Washington Press, 1999.

Connolly, William E. *Facing the Planetary: Entangled Humanism and the Politics of Swarming.* Durham, NC: Duke University Press, 2017.

Connolly, William E. *The Fragility of Things: Self-Organizing Processes, Neoliberal Fantasies, and Democratic Activism.* Durham, NC: Duke University Press, 2013.

Crapanzano, Vincent. *Imaginative Horizons: An Essay in Literary-Philosophical Anthropology.* Chicago: University of Chicago Press, 2004.

da Col, Giovanni. "Strathern Bottle: On Topology, Ethnographic Theory, and the

Method of Wonder." In *Hau Masterclass Series*, vol. 2, vii–xvi. Manchester, UK: Hau Society for Ethnographic Theory.

Daniel, E. Valentine. *Charred Lullabies: Chapters in an Anthropography of Violence.* Princeton, NJ: Princeton University Press, 1996.

Daston, Lorraine. "On Scientific Observation." *Isis* 99, no. 1 (2008): 97–110.

Daston, Lorraine, and Peter Galison. *Objectivity.* New York: Zone, 2007.

Davis, Heather, and Etienne Turpin, editors. *Art in the Anthropocene: Encounters among Aesthetics, Politics, Environments, and Epistemologies.* London: Open Humanities, 2015.

Debaene, Vincent. *Far Afield: French Anthropology between Science and Literature.* Chicago: University of Chicago Press, 2014.

Decker, Julie. *Gyre: The Plastic Ocean.* London: Booth-Clibborn, 2014.

Delaney, Carol. "The Meaning of Paternity and the Virgin Birth Debate." *Man* 21, no. 3 (1986): 494–513.

De León, Jason. *The Land of Open Graves: Living and Dying on the Migrant Trail.* Berkeley: University of California Press, 2015.

Deleuze, Gilles. *Cinema 2: The Time-Image.* Minneapolis: University of Minnesota Press, 1989.

Deleuze, Gilles. *Difference and Repetition.* London: Continuum, 2004.

Deleuze, Gilles, and Félix Guattari. *What Is Philosophy?* New York: Columbia University Press, 1994.

Denby, David. "Herder: Culture, Anthropology and the Enlightenment." *History of the Human Sciences* 18, no. 1 (2005): 55–76.

Descartes, René. *Meditations on First Philosophy.* Translated by John Cottingham. Cambridge: Cambridge University Press, 1996.

Descola, Philippe. *Beyond Nature and Culture.* Translated by Janet Lloyd. Chicago: University of Chicago Press, 2013.

Desjarlais, Robert, and C. Jason Throop. "Phenomenological Approaches in Anthropology." *Annual Review of Anthropology* 40 (2011): 87–102.

Dewey, John. *Art as Experience.* New York: Penguin, 1934.

Dillon, Grace. *Walking the Clouds: An Anthology of Indigenous Science Fiction.* Tucson: University of Arizona Press, 2012.

Dilthey, Wilhelm. *Selected Writings.* Translated by H. P. Rickman. Cambridge: Cambridge University Press, 1976.

Dirks, Nicholas. *Castes of Mind: Colonialism and the Making of Modern India.* Princeton, NJ: Princeton University Press, 2001.

Downie, R. Angus. *James George Frazer: The Portrait of a Scholar.* London: Watts & Co., 1940.

Draaisma, Douwe. *Metaphors of Memory: A History of Ideas about the Mind.* Cambridge: Cambridge University Press, 2000.

Evans-Pritchard, E. E. *Witchcraft, Oracles, and Magic among the Azande.* Oxford: Clarendon, 1976.

Fanon, Frantz. *The Wretched of the Earth.* New York: Grove, 1961.

Fassin, Didier. "The Endurance of Critique." *Anthropological Theory* 17, no. 1 (2017): 4–29.

Fassin, Didier. "Inequality of Lives, Hierarchies of Humanity: Moral Commitments and Ethical Dilemmas of Humanitarianism." In *In the Name of Humanity: The Government of Threat and Care*, edited by Ilana Feldman and Miriam Ticktin, 238–55. Durham, NC: Duke University Press, 2010.

Fassin, Didier. "Introduction: When Ethnography Goes Public." In *If Truth Be Told: The Politics of Public Ethnography*, edited by Didier Fassin, 1–16. Durham, NC: Duke University Press, 2017.

Feldman, Ilana, and Miriam Ticktin. "Government and Humanity." In *In the Name of Humanity: The Government of Threat and Care*, edited by Ilana Feldman and Miriam Ticktin, 1–26. Durham, NC: Duke University Press, 2010.

Fischer, Michael M. J. *Anthropological Futures*. Durham, NC: Duke University Press, 2009.

Forsdick, Charles. "*De la plume comme des pieds*: The Essay as a Peripatetic Genre." In *The Modern Essay in French: Movement, Instability, Performance*, edited by Charles Forsdick and Andrew Stafford, 45–60. Oxford: Peter Lang, 2005.

Forster, Michael. "Herder and the Birth of Modern Anthropology." In *After Herder: Philosophy of Language in the German Tradition*, 199–243. New York: Oxford University Press, 2010.

Foster, Hal. "The Artist as Ethnographer?" In *The Traffic in Culture: Refiguring Art and Anthropology*, edited by George Marcus and Fred Myers, 302–9. Berkeley: University of California Press, 1995.

Foucault, Michel. "Interview with Michel Foucault." In *Power*, edited by James Faubion, 239–97. New York: New Press, 2000.

Foucault, Michel. "The Masked Philosopher." In *Ethics: Subjectivity and Truth*, edited by Paul Rabinow, 321–28. New York: New Press, 1994.

Foucault, Michel. "What Is Critique?" In *The Politics of Truth*, edited by Sylvère Lotringer, 41–81. Los Angeles: Semiotext(e), 1997.

Foucault, Michel. "What Is Enlightenment?" In *Ethics: Subjectivity and Truth*, edited by Paul Rabinow, 303–19. New York: New Press, 1994.

Freedman, Carl, editor. *Conversations with Ursula K. Le Guin*. Jackson: University Press of Mississippi, 2008.

Freire-Marreco, Barbara, and John Linton Myres. *Notes and Queries on Anthropology*. Fourth edition. London: Royal Anthropological Institute, 1912.

Garcia, Angela. *The Pastoral Clinic: Addiction and Dispossession along the Rio Grande*. Berkeley: University of California Press, 2010.

Gates, Henry Louis. "A Negro Way of Saying." *New York Times*, April 21, 1985.

Geertz, Clifford. *Works and Lives: The Anthropologist as Author*. Stanford, CA: Stanford University Press, 1988.

Ginsberg, Daniel. "AAA Members outside the Academy: 2016 Membership Survey, Report #2." July 27, 2016. Arlington, VA: American Anthropological Association.

Ginsberg, Daniel. "Students Look toward the Job Market: 2016 Membership Survey, Report #4." October 3, 2016. Arlington, VA: American Anthropological Association.

Gupta, Akhil, and James Ferguson. "Discipline and Practice: 'The Field' as Site, Method, and Location in Anthropology." In *Anthropological Locations: Boundaries and Grounds of a Field Science*, edited by Akhil Gupta and James Ferguson, 1–46. Berkeley: University of California Press, 1997.

Gusterson, Hugh. "Homework: Toward a Critical Ethnography of the University." *American Ethnologist* 44, no. 3 (2017): 435–50.

Guyer, Jane. *Marginal Gains: Monetary Transactions in Atlantic Africa.* Chicago: University of Chicago Press, 2004.

Guyer, Jane. "'The Quickening of the Unknown': Epistemologies of Surprise in Anthropology." *Hau* 3, no. 3 (2013): 283–307.

Haraway, Donna. *Staying with the Trouble: Making Kin in the Chthulucene.* Durham, NC: Duke University Press, 2016.

Harrison, Faye V. *Outsider Within: Reworking Anthropology in the Global Age.* Urbana: University of Illinois Press, 2008.

Hayles, N. Katherine. *How We Became Posthuman: Virtual Bodies in Cybernetics, Literature, and Informatics.* Chicago: University of Chicago Press, 1999.

Helmreich, Stefan. "Nature/Culture/Seawater." *American Anthropologist* 113, no. 1 (2011): 132–44.

Herder, Johann Gottfried. *On World History: An Anthology.* Edited by Hans Adler and Ernest Menze. Armonk, NY: M. E. Sharpe, 1997.

Herder, Johann Gottfried. *Outlines of a Philosophy of the History of Man.* Translated by T. Churchill. New York: Bergman, 1966.

Herder, Johann Gottfried. *Philosophical Writings.* Translated and edited by Michael Forster. Cambridge: Cambridge University Press, 2002.

Hernandez, Graciela. "Multiple Subjectivities and Strategic Positionality: Zora Neale Hurston's Experimental Ethnographies." In *Women Writing Culture*, edited by Ruth Behar and Deborah A. Gordon, 148–65. Berkeley: University of California Press, 1995.

Hiddleston, Jane. "Aimé Césaire and Postcolonial Humanism." *Modern Language Review* 105 (2010): 87–102.

Hoffmann, Nigel. "The Unity of Science and Art: Goethean Phenomenology as a New Ecological Discipline." In *Goethe's Way of Science: A Phenomenology of Nature*, edited by David Seamon and Arthur Zajonc, 129–76. Albany: SUNY Press, 1998.

Holbraad, Martin. "Critique, Risqué: A Comment on Didier Fassin." *Anthropological Theory* 17, no. 2 (2017): 274–78.

Howell, Nancy. *Surviving Fieldwork: A Report of the Advisory Panel on Health and Safety in Fieldwork.* Washington, DC: American Anthropological Association, 1990.

Hurston, Zora Neale. *Barracoon: The Story of the Last "Black Cargo."* Edited by Deborah G. Plant. New York: HarperCollins, 2018.

Hurston, Zora Neale. *Dust Tracks on a Road.* In *Zora Neale Hurston: Folklore, Memoirs, and Other Writings*, edited by Cheryl Wall, 557–808. New York: Library of America, 1995.

Hurston, Zora Neale. *Mules and Men.* Philadelphia: J. B. Lippincott, 1935.

Hurston, Zora Neale. *Tell My Horse.* In *Zora Neale Hurston: Folklore, Memoirs, and Other Writings*, edited by Cheryl Wall, 269–556. New York: Library of America, 1995.

Hurston, Zora Neale. *Their Eyes Were Watching God.* New York: Harper Perennial, 1990.

Hurston, Zora Neale. "What White Publishers Won't Print." In *Zora Neale Hurston: Folklore, Memoirs, and Other Writings*, edited by Cheryl Wall, 950–55. New York: Library of America, 1995.

Hustak, Carla, and Natasha Myers. "Involutionary Momentum: Affective Ecologies and the Sciences of Plant/Insect Encounters." *Differences* 23, no. 3 (2012): 74–118.

Ingold, Tim. "Anthropology beyond Humanity." *Suomen Antropologi* 38, no. 3 (2013): 5–23.

Ingold, Tim. *Being Alive: Essays on Movement, Knowledge, and Description*. New York: Routledge, 2011.

Ingold, Tim. "That's Enough about Ethnography." *Hau* 4, no. 1 (2014): 383–95.

Jackson, Michael. *The Accidental Anthropologist*. Dunedin, NZ: Longacre, 2006.

Jackson, Michael. *Latitudes of Exile: Poems 1965–1975*. Dunedin, NZ: McIndoe, 1976.

Jackson, Michael. *The Other Shore: Essays on Writers and Writing*. Berkeley: University of California Press, 2013.

Jackson, Michael. *Paths toward a Clearing: Radical Empiricism and Ethnographic Inquiry*. Bloomington: Indiana University Press, 1989.

Jacobs, Karen. "From 'Spy-Glass' to 'Horizon': Tracking the Anthropological Gaze in Zora Neale Hurston." *Novel: A Forum on Fiction* 30, no. 3 (1997): 329–60.

James, William. *Essays in Radical Empiricism*. Lincoln: University of Nebraska Press, 1996.

James, William. *Pragmatism: A New Name for Some Old Ways of Thinking*. New York: Longmans, Green, 1925.

Jay, Martin. *Songs of Experience: Modern American and European Variations on a Universal Theme*. Berkeley: University of California Press, 2005.

Jensen, Casper Bruun. "Continuous Variations: The Conceptual and the Empirical in STS." *Science, Technology, and Human Values* 39, no. 2 (2014): 192–213.

Jones, Graham. *Magic's Reason: An Anthropology of Analogy*. Chicago: University of Chicago Press, 2017.

Kant, Immanuel. *Anthropology from a Pragmatic Point of View*. Translated by Robert Louden. Cambridge: Cambridge University Press, 2006.

Kaplan, Carla, editor. *Zora Neale Hurston: A Life in Letters*. New York: Anchor, 2003.

Kirksey, Eben, and Stefan Helmreich. "The Emergence of Multispecies Ethnography." *Cultural Anthropology* 25, no. 4 (2010): 545–76.

Kohn, Eduardo. "Ecopolitics." In *Lexicon for an Anthropocene Yet Unseen*, edited by Cymene Howe and Anand Pandian. New York: Punctum, 2019.

Kohn, Eduardo. *How Forests Think: Toward an Anthropology beyond the Human*. Berkeley: University of California Press, 2013.

Kozaitis, Kathryn. "Anthropological Praxis in Higher Education." *Annals of Anthropological Practice* 37, no. 1 (2013): 133–55.

Kroeber, Theodora. *Ishi in Two Worlds: A Biography of the Last Wild Indian in North America*. Berkeley: University of California Press, 1976.

Kuklick, Henrika. "Personal Equations: Reflections on the History of Fieldwork, with Special Reference to Sociocultural Anthropology." *Isis* 102 (2011): 1–33.

Kullberg, Christina. *The Poetics of Ethnography in Martinican Narratives: Exploring the Self and Environment*. Charlottesville: University of Virginia Press, 2013.

Latour, Bruno. "Anthropology at the Time of the Anthropocene: A Personal View of What Is to Be Studied." Distinguished Lecture, annual meeting of the American Anthropological Association, Washington, DC, December 2014.

Latour, Bruno. *An Inquiry into Modes of Existence*. Cambridge, MA: Harvard University Press, 2013.

Leach, Edmund. "The Epistemological Background to Malinowski's Empiricism." In *Man and Culture: An Evaluation of the Work of Bronislaw Malinowski*, 119–37. London: Routledge and Kegan Paul, 1957.

Leach, James. *Creative Land: Place and Procreation on the Rai Coast of Papua New Guinea*. New York: Berghahn, 2003.

Le Guin, Ursula K. *The Dispossessed*. New York: Avon, 1974.

Le Guin, Ursula K. *The Language of the Night: Essays on Fantasy and Science Fiction*. New York: Putnam, 1979.

Le Guin, Ursula K. *The Left Hand of Darkness*. New York: Ace, 1969.

Le Guin, Ursula K. *The Telling*. New York: Harcourt, 2000.

Le Guin, Ursula K. *The Wave in the Mind: Talks and Essays on the Writer, the Reader, and the Imagination*. Boston: Shambhala, 2004.

Le Guin, Ursula K. *Worlds of Exile and Illusion*. New York: Orb, 1996.

Lévi-Strauss, Claude. "Jean-Jacques Rousseau, Founder of the Sciences of Man." In *Structural Anthropology*, vol. 2, 33–43. London: Allen Lane, 1976.

Lévi-Strauss, Claude. *The Naked Man*. Chicago: University of Chicago Press, 1981.

Lévi-Strauss, Claude. *The Raw and the Cooked*. Chicago: University of Chicago Press, 1987.

Lévi-Strauss, Claude. *Tristes Tropiques*. New York: Penguin, 1992.

Lévi-Strauss, Claude. *The View from Afar*. Chicago: University of Chicago Press, 1992.

Longobardi, Pam. *Drifters: Plastic, Pollution, and Personhood*. Milan: Charta, 2009.

Mach, Ernst. *Knowledge and Error: Sketches on the Psychology of Enquiry*. Dordrecht: D. Reidel, 1976.

Mach, Ernst. *Popular Scientific Lectures*. Translated by Thomas McCormack. Chicago: Open Court, 1895.

Malinowski, Bronisław. *Argonauts of the Western Pacific*. Prospect Heights, IL: Waveland, 1984.

Malinowski, Bronisław. "Baloma: The Spirits of the Dead in the Trobriand Islands." *Journal of the Royal Anthropological Institute of Great Britain and Ireland* 46 (1916): 353–430.

Malinowski, Bronisław. *Coral Gardens and Their Magic: A Study of the Methods of Tilling the Soil and of Agricultural Rites in the Trobriand Islands*. 2 vols. New York: Dover, 1935.

Malinowski, Bronisław. *A Diary in the Strict Sense of the Term*. Stanford, CA: Stanford University Press, 1989.

Malinowski, Bronisław. *Freedom and Civilization*. Bloomington: Indiana University Press, 1944.

Malinowski, Bronisław. *Magic, Science, and Religion and Other Essays*. Boston: Beacon, 1948.

Malinowski, Bronisław. *Myth in Primitive Psychology*. New York: W. W. Norton, 1926.

Malinowski, Bronisław. "On the Principle of the Economy of Thought." In *The Early Writings of Bronislaw Malinowski*, edited by Robert Thornton and Peter Skalnik, 89–116. Cambridge: Cambridge University Press, 2011.

Malinowski, Bronisław. "The Rationalization of Anthropology and Administration." *Africa* 3, no. 4 (1930): 405–30.

Malm, Andreas, and Alf Hornborg. "The Geology of Mankind: A Critique of the Anthropocene Narrative." *Anthropocene Review* 1, no. 1 (2014): 62–69.

Maniglier, Patrice. "L'humanisme interminable de Claude Lévi-Strauss." *Les Temps Modernes* 609 (2000): 216–41.

Marcus, George. "Notes toward an Ethnographic Memoir of Supervising Graduate Research through Anthropology's Decades of Transformation." In *Fieldwork Is Not What It Used to Be: Learning Anthropology's Method in a Time of Transition*, edited by James Faubion and George Marcus, 1–31. Ithaca, NY: Cornell University Press, 2009.

Marcus, George, and Michael M. J. Fischer. *Anthropology as Cultural Critique: An Experimental Moment in the Human Sciences*. Chicago: University of Chicago Press, 1986.

Markus, Gyorgy. "Culture: The Making and the Make-Up of a Concept (an Essay in Historical Semantics)." *Dialectical Anthropology* 18, no. 1 (1993): 3–29.

Massumi, Brian. "On Critique." *Inflexions* 4 (December 2010): 337–40.

Mazzarella, William. *The Mana of Mass Society*. Chicago: University of Chicago Press, 2017.

McLean, Stuart. *Fictionalizing Anthropology: Encounters and Fabulations at the Edges of the Human*. Minneapolis: University of Minnesota Press, 2017.

Mead, Margaret. "Apprenticeship under Boas." In *The Anthropology of Franz Boas: Essays on the Centennial of His Birth*, edited by Walter Goldschmidt, 29–45. San Francisco: American Anthropological Association, 1959.

Mead, Margaret. *Blackberry Winter: My Earlier Years*. London: Angus and Robertson, 1973.

Miner, Horace. "Body Ritual among the Nacirema." *American Anthropologist* 58, no. 3 (1956): 503–7.

Mitchell, W. J. T. "The Commitment to Form; or, Still Crazy after All These Years." *PMLA* 118, no. 2 (2003): 321–25.

Muthu, Sankar. *Enlightenment against Empire*. Princeton, NJ: Princeton University Press, 2003.

Myers, Natasha. "Conversations on Plant Sensing: Notes from the Field." *NatureCulture* 3 (2015): 35–66.

Myers, Natasha. *Rendering Life Molecular: Models, Modelers, and Excitable Matter*. Durham, NC: Duke University Press, 2015.

Narayan, Kirin. *Alive in the Writing: Crafting Ethnography in the Company of Chekhov*. Chicago: University of Chicago Press, 2012.

Nietzsche, Friedrich. *The Gay Science*. Translated by Walter Kaufmann. New York: Vintage, 1974.

Ntarangwi, Mwenda. *Reversed Gaze: An African Ethnography of American Anthropology*. Urbana: University of Illinois Press, 2010.

Ortner, Sherry. "Dark Anthropology and Its Others: Theory since the Eighties." *Hau* 6, no. 1 (2016): 47–73.

Pandian, Anand. *Crooked Stalks: Cultivating Virtue in South India*. Durham, NC: Duke University Press, 2009.

Pandian, Anand. "Open Access, Open Minds." Dispatches, *Cultural Anthropology* website, June 15, 2018. https://culanth.org/fieldsights/1455-open-access-open-minds.

Pandian, Anand. *Reel World: An Anthropology of Creation*. Durham, NC: Duke University Press, 2015.

Pandian, Anand. "The Time of Anthropology: Notes from a Field of Contemporary Experience." *Cultural Anthropology* 27, no. 4 (2012): 547–71.

Pandian, Anand, and M. P. Mariappan. *Ayya's Accounts: A Ledger of Hope in Modern India*. Bloomington: Indiana University Press, 2014.

Pandian, Anand, and M. P. Mariappan. *Mitcham Meethi, Oru Anubava Kanakku*. Chennai: Kalachuvadu, 2012.

Pandian, Anand, and Stuart McLean, editors. *Crumpled Paper Boat: Experiments in Ethnographic Writing*. Durham, NC: Duke University Press, 2017.

Peluso, Nancy Lee. "Coercing Conservation? The Politics of State Resource Control." *Global Environmental Change* 3, no. 2 (1993): 199–217.

Platzer, David, and Anne Allison. "Academic Precarity in American Anthropology." Dispatches, *Cultural Anthropology* website, February 12, 2018. https://culanth.org/fieldsights/1310-academic-precarity-in-american-anthropology.

Povinelli, Elizabeth. "Fires, Fogs, Winds." *Cultural Anthropology* 32, no. 4 (2017): 504–13.

Povinelli, Elizabeth. "The Will to Be Otherwise / The Effort of Endurance." *South Atlantic Quarterly* 111, no. 3 (2012): 453–75.

Powdermaker, Hortense. *Stranger and Friend: The Way of an Anthropologist*. New York: W. W. Norton, 1966.

Price, David. *Cold War Anthropology: The CIA, the Pentagon, and the Growth of Dual Use Anthropology*. Durham, NC: Duke University Press, 2016.

Price, David. "One Who Raged against the Machine." *Counterpunch*, February 19, 2014. https://www.counterpunch.org/2014/02/19/one-who-raged-against-the-machine/.

Rabinow, Paul. *Anthropos Today: Reflections on Modern Equipment*. Princeton, NJ: Princeton University Press, 2003.

Raffles, Hugh. "Twenty-Five Years Is a Long Time." *Cultural Anthropology* 27, no. 3 (2012): 526–34.

Raheja, Gloria Goodwin, and Ann Grodzins Gold. *Listen to the Heron's Words: Reimagining Gender and Kinship in North India*. Berkeley: University of California Press, 1994.

Rahman, Tariq. "The Precarity of Academic Work, the Work of Academic Precarity." Dialogues, *Cultural Anthropology* website, March 21, 2018. https://culanth.org/fieldsights/1338-the-precarity-of-academic-work-the-work-of-academic-precarity.

Rancière, Jacques. *The Ignorant Schoolmaster: Five Lessons in Intellectual Emancipation*. Stanford, CA: Stanford University Press, 1991.

Reno, Joshua. *Waste Away: Working and Living with a North American Landfill*. Berkeley: University of California Press, 2015.

Rheinberger, Hans-Jorg. "The Art of Exploring the Unknown: Views on Contemporary Research in the Life Sciences." In *Science as Cultural Practice*, edited by Moritz Epple and Claus Zittel, vol. 1, 141–52. Berlin: Akademie, 2010.

Ribeiro, Gustavo Lins. "World Anthropologies: Anthropological Cosmopolitanisms and Cosmopolitics." *Annual Review of Anthropology* 43 (2014): 483–98.

Robeson, Eslanda Goode. *African Journey.* New York: John Day, 1945.

Rosaldo, Renato. *The Day of Shelly's Death: The Poetry and Ethnography of Grief.* Durham, NC: Duke University Press, 2013.

Sagan, Dorion. "The Human Is More Than Human: Interspecies Communities and the New 'Facts of Life.'" *Cultural Anthropology* website, April 24, 2011. https://culanth .org/fieldsights/228-the-human-is-more-than-human-interspecies-communities-and -the-new-facts-of-life.

Samuels, Maru. "Global Conservation Problem Is in the Photos." September 7, 2016. https://www.linkedin.com/pulse/global-conservation-problem-photos-maru-samuels/.

Sawyer, Suzana, and Arun Agrawal. "Environmental Orientalisms." *Cultural Critique* 45 (2000): 71–108.

Scheper-Hughes, Nancy. "The Primacy of the Ethical: Propositions for a Militant Anthropology." *Current Anthropology* 36, no. 3 (1995): 409–40.

Schneider, Arnd, and Christopher Wright. "The Challenge of Practice." In *Contemporary Art and Anthropology*, edited by Arnd Schneider and Christopher Wright, 1–28. Oxford: Berg, 2006.

Scott, Joan W. 1991. "The Evidence of Experience." *Critical Inquiry* 17, no. 4 (1991): 773–97.

Scranton, Roy. *Learning to Die in the Anthropocene: Reflections on the End of a Civilization.* San Francisco: City Lights, 2015.

Shapiro, Nicholas, and Eben Kirksey. "Chemo-Ethnography: An Introduction." *Cultural Anthropology* 32, no. 4 (2017): 481–93.

Shore, Cris. "Fictions of Fieldwork: Depicting the 'Self' in Ethnographic Writing." In *Being There: Fieldwork in Anthropology*, edited by C. W. Watson, 25–48. London: Pluto, 1999.

Sikka, Sonia. *Herder on Humanity and Cultural Difference: Enlightened Relativism.* Cambridge: Cambridge University Press, 2011.

Singh, Bhrigupati, and Jane Guyer. "A Joyful History of Anthropology." *Hau* 6, no. 2 (2016): 197–211.

Sontag, Susan. *Against Interpretation.* New York: Picador, 1966.

Speakman, Robert J., Carla S. Hadden, Matthew H. Colvin, Justin Cramb, K. C. Jones, Travis W. Jones, et al. "Market Share and Recent Hiring Trends in Anthropology Faculty Positions." *PLOS ONE* 13, no. 9 (2018): e0202528.

Stein, Felix. "Anthropology's 'Impact': A Comment on Audit and the Unmeasurable Nature of Critique." *Journal of the Royal Anthropological Association* 24 (2017): 10–29.

Stengers, Isabelle. "The Cosmopolitical Proposal." In *Making Things Public: Atmospheres of Democracy*, edited by Bruno Latour and Peter Weibel, 994–1003. Cambridge, MA: MIT Press, 2005.

Stevenson, Lisa. *Life Beside Itself: Imagining Care in the Canadian Arctic.* Berkeley: University of California Press, 2014.

Stewart, Kathleen. *Ordinary Affects*. Durham, NC: Duke University Press, 2007.

Stocking, George. "The Ethnographer's Magic: Fieldwork in British Anthropology from Tylor to Malinowski." In *Observers Observed: Essays on Ethnographic Fieldwork*, edited by George Stocking, 70–120. Madison: University of Wisconsin Press, 1983.

Stone, Nomi. "Aesthetics and Politics: A Reaction to 'War Poem' as Film." 2018. http://motionpoems.org/episode/war-poem/bonus/.

Stone, Nomi. *Kill Class*. North Adams, MA: Tupelo, 2019.

Stone, Nomi. "Living the Laughscream: Human Technology and Affective Maneuvers in the Iraq War." *Cultural Anthropology* 32, no. 1 (2017): 149–74.

Strathern, Marilyn. *The Gender of the Gift: Problems with Women and Problems with Society in Melanesia*. Berkeley: University of California Press, 1988.

Strathern, Marilyn. "No Nature, No Culture: The Hagen Case." In *Nature, Culture and Gender*, edited by Carol MacCormack and Marilyn Strathern, 174–222. Cambridge: Cambridge University Press, 1980.

Strathern, Marilyn. "Out of Context: The Persuasive Fictions of Anthropology." *Current Anthropology* 28, no. 3 (1987): 251–81.

Strathern, Marilyn. *Partial Connections*. Walnut Creek, CA: AltaMira, 2004.

TallBear, Kim. "Pipestone Relations: Carvers, Scientists, and Bureaucrats." Paper presented at the annual meeting of the American Anthropological Association, Minneapolis, MN, November 19, 2016.

Taussig, Karen-Sue, Klaus Hoeyer, and Stefan Helmreich. "The Anthropology of Potentiality in Biomedicine." *Current Anthropology* 54, suppl. 7 (2013): S3–S14.

Taussig, Michael. *What Color Is the Sacred?* Chicago: University of Chicago Press, 2009.

Thoreau, Henry David. "Walking." In *Walden and Other Writings of Henry David Thoreau*, edited by Brooks Atkinson, 595–632. New York: Modern Library, 1937.

Todd, Zoe. "The Decolonial Turn 2.0: The Reckoning." *Anthro{dendum}*, June 15, 2018. https://anthrodendum.org/2018/06/15/the-decolonial-turn-2-0-the-reckoning/.

Todd, Zoe. "Re-situating Alberta as a 'Fish-Place': Human-Fish Relations and Indigenous Legal Orders in Prairie Decolonial Resistance." Paper presented at the annual meeting of the American Anthropological Association, Minneapolis, MN, November 19, 2016.

Todd, Zoe. "Should I Stay or Should I Go?" *Anthro{dendum}*, May 12, 2018. https://anthrodendum.org/2018/05/12/should-i-stay-or-should-i-go/.

Tsing, Anna. "More-Than-Human Sociality: A Call for Critical Description." In *Anthropology and Nature*, edited by Kirsten Hastrup, 27–42. New York: Routledge, 2013.

Tsing, Anna. *The Mushroom at the End of the World: On the Possibility of Life in Capitalist Ruins*. Princeton, NJ: Princeton University Press, 2015.

Tumarkin, Daniel. "Miklouho-Maclay: 19th Century Russian Anthropologist and Humanist." *RAIN* 51 (1982): 4–7.

Turner, Victor. "Experience and Performance: Towards a New Processual Anthropology." In *On the Edge of the Bush: Anthropology as Experience*. Tucson: University of Arizona Press, 1985.

Tyler, Steven A. "Post-modern Ethnography: From Document of the Occult to Occult Document." In *Writing Culture: The Poetics and Politics of Ethnography*, edited by

James Clifford and George E. Marcus, 98–121. Berkeley: University of California Press, 1986.

UNEP World Conservation Monitoring Centre and International Union for Conservation of Nature. *Protected Planet Report 2016.* Cambridge, UK, and Gland, Switzerland: UNEP-WCMC and IUCN, 2016.

Verran, Helen. "Staying True to the Laughter in Nigerian Classrooms." *The Sociological Review* 47 (1999): 136–55.

Viveiros de Castro, Eduardo. *Cannibal Metaphysics: For a Post-structural Anthropology.* Edited and translated by Peter Skafish. Minneapolis, MN: Univocal, 2014.

Viveiros de Castro, Eduardo. "Zeno and the Art of Anthropology: Of Lies, Beliefs, Paradoxes, and Other Truths." *Common Knowledge* 17, no. 1 (2011): 128–45.

Wagner, Roy. *An Anthropology of the Subject: Holographic Worldview in New Guinea and Its Meaning and Significance for the World of Anthropology.* Berkeley: University of California Press, 2001.

Wagner, Roy. *The Invention of Culture.* Chicago: University of Chicago Press, 1981.

Walley, Christine. *Rough Waters: Nature and Development in an East African Marine Park.* Princeton, NJ: Princeton University Press, 2004.

Wayne, Helena. *The Story of a Marriage: The Letters of Bronislaw Malinowski and Elsie Masson, Volume 1, 1916–20.* New York: Routledge, 1995.

Welch-Devine, Meredith, and Lisa M. Campbell. "Sorting Out Roles and Defining Divides: Social Sciences at the World Conservation Congress." *Conservation and Society* 8, no. 4 (2010): 339–48.

West, Paige. *Conservation Is Our Government Now: The Politics of Ecology in Papua New Guinea.* Durham, NC: Duke University Press, 2006.

Whittall, Arnold. "The Music." In *Richard Wagner, Parsifal,* by Lucy Beckett, 61–86. Cambridge: Cambridge University Press, 1981.

Wilcken, Patrick. *Claude Lévi-Strauss: The Poet in the Laboratory.* New York: Penguin, 2010.

Wilder, Gary. "Radical Humanism and Black Atlantic Criticism." Talk given in the Department of Anthropology Colloquium Series, Johns Hopkins University, Baltimore, MD, April 26, 2016.

Williams, Raymond. *Keywords.* Oxford: Oxford University Press, 1976.

Williams, Raymond. *Marxism and Literature.* Oxford: Oxford University Press, 1977.

Wiseman, Boris. *Lévi-Strauss, Anthropology, and Aesthetics.* Cambridge: Cambridge University Press, 2007.

Wolf, Eric. *Anthropology.* Englewood Cliffs, NJ: Prentice-Hall, 1964.

Young, Michael W. *Malinowski: Odyssey of an Anthropologist, 1884–1920.* Vol. 1. New Haven, CT: Yale University Press, 2004.

Zalasiewicz, Jan, et al. "The Geological Cycle of Plastics and Their Use as a Stratigraphic Indicator of the Anthropocene." *Anthropocene* 13, no. 1 (2016): 4–17.

Zammito, John. "Epigenesis: Concept and Metaphor in Herder's *Ideen.*" In *Vom Selbstdenken: Aufklärung und Aufklärungskritik in Johann Gottfried Herder's Ideen zur Philosophie der Geschichte der Menschheit,* edited by Rudolf Otto and John Zammito, 131–45. Heidelberg: Synchron, 2001.

Zammito, John. *Kant, Herder, and the Birth of Anthropology*. Chicago: University of Chicago Press, 2002.

Zhan, Mei. "The Empirical as Conceptual: Transdisciplinary Engagements with an 'Experiential Medicine.'" *Science, Technology and Human Values* 39, no. 2 (2014): 236–63.

Zilcosky, John. "Poetry after Auschwitz? Celan and Adorno Revisited." *Deutsche Vierteljahrsschrift für Literaturwissenschaft und Geistesgeschichte* 79 (2005): 670–91.

INDEX